Praise for

WITHOUT A WORD

"We know through our own experience of having a son with autism that challenges also present many blessings. We admire the fact that Jim and Jill have been willing to share both their struggles and successes with the world. This story is a tribute to Hunter James Kelly. Hunter's short life transformed the Kelly family, and through the work of Hunter's Hope, the foundation that bears his name, his life will touch countless other families. Reading this book was like watching a miracle unfold."

—Dan and Claire Marino

"Jim and Jill Kelly were always headed toward greatness. Who knew that a Hall of Fame career with the Buffalo Bills would be dwarfed by their son, Hunter? This is a story that refuses to detail a sadness that would seem only natural. Instead, it is an uplifting tale of courage, hope, and love. We are proud to call the Kelly family our friends. You will, too!"

—Chris and Katherine Berman

"The story of the Kelly family is painful, but it is not a story of pain. It's a story of redemption, grace, reconciliation, and the powerful activity of the work-all-things-for-good God. I found myself left without a word as I read it—humbled by the courage of Hunter, the love of his sisters, and the indescribable way that God demonstrated His love to Jim and Jill. Their story has served to enflame my faith, and it will yours as well."

—Dr. Jerry Gillis, lead pastor, the Chapel
at CrossPoint, Buffalo, NY

"I was emotionally drained but inspired when I read Jill's book. God's timing was perfect. This wonderful book helped me to see my own 'trials' in a completely different light."

—Denise Jackson, author of the
#1 *New York Times* bestseller *It's All About Him*

"WITHOUT A WORD was more than a book to my husband and me. It was an education on faith. We could say being personal friends with the Kelly family gave us an inspirational edge, but we would be lying. This book takes you far beyond the confinements of friendship and even family. Jill Kelly embarks with you on her journey of love and heartache, the heartache that only a mother blessed with a terminally ill child can take you on, yet you remain inspired through her pain. Jill masterfully engages us with her words and is able to act as a literary surgeon of sorts. She performs the feat of opening your heart and then proceeds to place her innermost feelings right inside you. She then beautifully sews you back up so you'll never lose the experience that the two of you just shared, nor feel pain from the wounds of her story. Needless to say, you will never be the same. These words have changed your heart forever. You now have a heart that beats harmoniously with that of a graciously blessed child. By the end of WITHOUT A WORD she will have achieved the task of allowing you to know her amazing son, Hunter. Jim and Jill Kelly unselfishly invite us all to have our hearts changed by Hunter's precious life, to be devastated by his early departure, and, finally, to be restored by the faith he left us with."   —Thurman and Patti Thomas

"WITHOUT A WORD, sweet and unyielding innocence interrupted the Kelly family lifestyle, so immersed in the demanding expectations of others. Without uttering a single phrase, Hunter Kelly came, lived, and departed having poignantly pioneered hope and rescue to the future lives and stories of thousands and thousands of families. Within the pages of this raw, honest, and tender revelation of intimate family ties, it is my prayer that you will feel the same emotions of joy, anguish, anger, heartache, thankfulness, forgiveness, and love that I have had the privilege to share with these very, very special friends. Because Hunter was such a precious gift from God, the Kelly family will never be the same. Due to reading this inspiring journey, neither will I, and neither will you."
          —Richard R. George, shepherding pastor of the Chapel at
          CrossPoint, counselor, freelance writer, playwright,
          poet, and conference speaker

"Jim and Jill Kelly have lived every family's best sports dream and every parent's worst nightmare. They've also faced every couple's greatest challenge. In WITHOUT A WORD, Jim and Jill open wide the doors of their home and their hearts and invite the rest of us inside to share the joy of having Hunter, the heartbreak of losing him, and the beautiful healing God has brought to their lives."
          —Nancy Guthrie, author of
          Hearing Jesus Speak Into Your Sorrow

Without a Word

How a Boy's Unspoken Love Changed Everything

211018

JILL KELLY

FaithWords

New York   Boston   Nashville

Unless otherwise indicated, Scriptures are taken from the Holy
Bible, *New International Version®, NIV®*. Copyright © 1973, 1978,
1984 by International Bible Society. Used by permission of Zondervan
Bible Publishers. All rights reserved worldwide.
Scriptures noted KJV are taken from the King James Version
of the Bible.

FaithWords
Hachette Book Group
237 Park Avenue
New York, NY 10017

www.faithwords.com

Printed in the United States of America

Originally published in hardcover by FaithWords.

First Trade Edition: September 2011
10 9 8 7 6 5 4 3 2 1

FaithWords is a division of Hachette Book Group, Inc.
The FaithWords name and logo are trademarks of Hachette Book
Group, Inc.

The publisher is not responsible for websites (or their content)
that are not owned by the publisher.

The Library of Congress has cataloged the
hardcover edition as follows:
Kelly, Jill.
    Without a word : how a boy's unspoken love changed everything /
Jill Kelly.—1st ed.
        p. cm.
    Summary: "Hunter Kelly, son of Jill and football great Jim Kelly, changed
their lives and the lives of countless others in his short, silent but powerful
life"—Provided by publisher.
    ISBN 978-0-446-56337-6
    1. Kelly, Hunter, 1997–2005.   2. Leukodystrophy, Globoid cell—Patients—
Biography.   3. Chronically ill children—United States—Biography.
4. Sons—United States—Biography.   5. Kelly, Jill—Family.   6. Kelly, Jim,
1960—Family.   7. Parent and child—United States.   8. Love.   9. Kelly,
Jill—Philosophy.   10. Christian biography—United States.   I. Title.
    RC394.L4K45 2010
    362.196'1540092—dc22
    [B]

                                                                2010006174

ISBN 978-0-446-56338-3 (pbk.)

Hunter James Kelly

February 14, 1997–August 5, 2005

Our lives are forever changed because of you.
Your bravery taught us to be bold.
Your courage made us strong.
Your humility inspired us.
Your hope encouraged us.
Your unspoken love changed us.
We thank God for your amazing life.
See you soon, little buddy.

I dedicate this book to my two daughters,
Erin Marie and Camryn Lynn.
Girls, this is for you so that you'll never forget how
God rescued our family and how the unspoken love
of your brother, Hunter, changed everything.
I love you girls so much!
We'll see Hunterboy before you know it.
I can't wait!

Contents

Foreword

Jim and Jill Kelly are some of the most courageous people we know. Their work through Hunter's Hope on behalf of terminally ill children living with Krabbe disease is as legendary as Jim's NFL career—and even tougher. Like the McGraws, the Kellys are all about the things that really matter in life: faith and family. There's nothing that brings us as much pleasure as our girls and each other. Our family is a blessing, a gift from God that we refuse to take for granted no matter how busy life gets.

This is a story of love and redemption, of dreams lost and dreams found, of light in the valley of the shadow of death. It's the story of their son, Hunter. And woven through its pages is a tapestry of joy, grief, pain, and healing as the Kellys willingly take you to a sacred place. A place hidden deep within the treasures of a parent's love for a terminally ill child. A place few of us, thank God, have had to go.

Hunter never threw the football his father longed to toss around with him. He was unable to give his mother the hugs and kisses she ached for. And he never wrestled around with or teased his two sisters. Yet he accomplished so much more than many of us ever will. His extraordinary bravery in the face of incredible suffering taught Jim, Jill, and their children life lessons they would not have learned otherwise. Lessons that healed the deepest of all wounds and saved a family.

We were profoundly moved by the courage it took Jim and Jill to be so agonizingly honest. It is rare to find people willing to be vulnerable enough to bare their souls and open their lives to all of us so completely. Yet they would admit that it was Hunter's courage that strengthened them, and his love that made them willing to risk loving deep enough to take us behind the closed doors of their marriage and family life.

We're very thankful Jim and Jill came into our lives. And through *Without a Word*, we know them in ways we never thought we would. Now you, too, share that privilege.

Forewords, like songs, are written in all kinds of shapes and sizes, and like a lot of songs, this one took on a life of its own. As a rule we have a few things to say, whether we sing them, write them, or speak them—but we're going to wrap it up here. You see, through reading this book, we've come to discover that sometimes you can say more—you can even say it all, just as Hunter did...

Without a word.

Tim McGraw and Faith Hill

Love endures where joy and sorrow meet.

—ANONYMOUS

Preface

Dear Reader,

This book contains my very heart, pieces of precious memories engraved on my soul. Memory is a very curious thing, isn't it? We remember what we wish we could forget and forget what we long to remember. And maybe, oddly, it's a good thing.

Without a Word draws you into moments I remember—moments that crushed my heart, moments covered in muck and mire, moments I wish had never happened and those I'd love to relive again, moments that add up to a time filled with indescribable joy and unimaginable pain. While for the most part this is a chronological account of my family's journey, *Without a Word* is more than that. There are journal entries and fragments of events and moments that changed my life, that changed our family—forever.

Maybe you'll be changed, too.

Jill Kelly

Without a Word

Prologue

Beyond Words

December 16, 2003

It's 4:00 in the morning, and in the predawn darkness I cling desperately to my son's hand as the respirator helps keep him alive. Hunter is struggling heroically to breathe but just seems too weak to respond. The overwhelming sense of dread is so heavy as I wonder if this latest struggle could break his will to fight.

My prayers are desperate, clumsy, and persistent as I willingly place my precious son in God's hands. There is nowhere else to turn, for I know the night-shift doctors and nurses have tried every intervention possible to help him breathe. As I quietly ponder the hope held in my heart, a sigh of relief escapes my lips as Hunter's fragile body resists surrender.

Keep fighting, little buddy, please keep fighting.

"Please do something, Lord. I love him. I need him."

Though we have walked down this scary path many times before, this night is different. It seems the only sounds in the hospital are coming from Hunter's room. Why is it so quiet tonight? Where is the usual night-shift hustle and bustle? Why can't I hear the routine beeps, drips, and alarms against the concerned conversations of the hospital staff? Everything around me is so still, far too still.

For some reason no one asks me about signing a DNR [Do Not Resuscitate] form. Maybe they finally got the message through the countless refusals we have given them. We will never sign those papers. Life is a precious gift, and as long as our little buddy has the will to fight for his, we will always do whatever it takes to help him.

Why are my mom and dad on vacation right now? My mother should be here; we need her. I feel so alone. As soon as she gets word that Hunter is in here, she'll be on the next flight home.

I hope.

Thank God, Jim is home with our girls; they're probably terrified. They love their brother so much. I wonder what they were thinking as policemen and emergency medical technicians whisked Mommy and Hunter off to the hospital. As the ambulance siren faded in the distance, I can only hope that Daddy's presence will be a comfort to them. I wish I could help them understand, but I don't even understand.

As I sit on Hunter's hospital bed and run my fingers through his soft, wavy hair, I cringe at the thought that he might not come off the respirator this time. The obnoxious squeaking of a gurney breaks into my troubling thoughts. As I turn, the body of a lifeless child covered from head to toe with a dingy hospital sheet goes by.

Who is that child? What happened to him…or her? My heart aches for the family of that precious little one. Why did I have to turn around at that very moment? Why are the doors to our room open? We always close our doors.

My eyes burn and fill with tears as I cradle Hunter's limp body and look into his beautiful yet fearful eyes. Realizing that I caught a glimpse of the lifeless child, the nurses rush to apologize. "You weren't supposed to see that, Mrs. Kelly," one says. "We're so sorry."

I imagine they become accustomed to death around here. Death is an ever-present shadow in the midst of life-giving technology, knowledge, and medicine. I can't help but wonder if that's how Hunter is going to leave the hospital this time—his beautiful angelic face and soft white body covered by a sheet?

It can't happen. This won't happen. No, Hunter will get better.

Tears pool and run down my cheeks, but I don't want Hunter to sense that I'm a total wreck so I quickly wipe them off—again. The realization that he hears me crying jolts me from my grief. I must stop, for his sake. Hunter cannot afford to be fearful. My strength must be resurrected for my son. We both need to be strong.

The desire to close my eyes is overwhelming. Exhaustion consumes me, but there's no time for sleep. I'm beyond sleep. Hunter needs me. Every move the doctors and nurses make must be monitored. He has to get better. We must do whatever it takes.

Watching my only son suffer is more painful than words can describe. And as I ache to take his place, even if just for a moment, the all-too-familiar, unanswerable question looms ever before me: Why does he have to go through all this? Why?

Yet in the midst of our family's anguish, somehow I know he'll make it home again, just as he has so many times before. He's such a brave little soldier. He'll come off that respirator and we'll be home for Christmas. He'll breathe again on his own. I just know he will.

And in that moment, there in Hunter's hospital room, as I hold my son, I begin to recall the extraordinary chain of events that brought me to this moment.

Chapter 1

Not What It Seems

January 21, 1997

It's hard to describe the emotions wrapped up in the day. After devoting heart, soul, and life to the game of football, my husband, Jim, had decided to hang up his football cleats. After four Super Bowl appearances, four AFC Championships, six AFC East Championships, and five Pro Bowl invitations, "K-Gun Kelly" would no longer lead the Buffalo Bills as their quarterback.

Throngs of teammates and fans as well as family members and friends filled the Buffalo Bills Fieldhouse on that brisk afternoon. I vividly remember walking through the back entrance and slowly making our way across the artificial turf to the front end of the building where the temporary platform and podium stood. It was impossible not to think about the countless hours that Jim had spent here.

It was also difficult to comprehend what our life would be like without football as the focus. My heart ached for Jim; his life had intimately revolved around this game since he was a boy, and now he was walking away. Football defined Jim—it defined our family. Our lives were consumed with the sport and the passionate man who played it so well: my husband. The more I thought about the uncertainty of the future, the more anxious I became. I didn't know what to say to Jim as we walked across the field, so I just held his hand.

Noisy chatter from fans and media anticipating Jim's farewell ceremony surrounded us as we approached the curtain behind the stage that separated Jim from his devoted well-wishers. Jim paused to compose himself before taking the stage and reviewed his speech one last time. Meanwhile, I watched and waited for our cue to enter the roped-off area.

It was an unprecedented moment. For years, Jim had calmly handled the weekly pressure and scrutiny associated with being the quarterback of the Bills, but at this point, he was a nervous wreck. However, he had gone over his retirement speech with the same fervor and energy he had once poured into studying his playbook and pregame film, so he was ready—just as he had been on all of those game-day Sundays when taking the field in front of eighty thousand diehard Buffalo Bills fans.

We were given the cue, and it was time. Time for Jim to walk away from the game he loved, the game he lived for each and every Sunday, the game that had shaped our family for so many years.

"Well, I guess this is it," Jim said solemnly as he took my hand.

We made our way up to the platform while hundreds of fans cheered and shouted.

"You're the best, Jimbo!" one man hollered.

"We'll miss you, Jim!" another shouted.

When the crowd of adoring enthusiasts finally quieted, we all listened intently as team owner Ralph Wilson and head coach Marv Levy made their opening remarks. Each talked about Jim's many accomplishments and expressed gratitude for the man who wore number 12. The heart and soul of the Buffalo Bills football team, my husband, Jim, was retiring. It just didn't seem real.

Especially since we knew Jim could still play and win. He was as tough, driven, and passionate as ever. Both Dan Marino and John Elway—Jim's fellow members of the NFL draft class of 1983—were still suiting up for their respective teams. But Bills management had determined that it was time for new direction at the quarterback position. Believing the franchise needed some younger blood, the Bills dynasty had regrouped and was looking for someone fresh to take the snaps. A new hero.

In his eleven seasons with the team, Jim had been that hero. He'd put Buffalo on the NFL map and brought life to the city and its thousands of fans with his gritty performances each Sunday. He had also grown to love Western New York and its people. So while other teams had expressed interest in Jim once the Bills had announced their decision, Jim wasn't about to pour his life into a new offense no matter how much they would pay him. His heart was sold out to Buffalo; no other team would do. And though it hurt deeply, Jim accepted the front office's decision with the same class, grace, and toughness that had characterized his career.

What would the Bills do now? I wondered. What would the city of Buffalo do? What would Jim do? With so many questions running through my mind, I could only imagine what was going through Jim's.

As he began his retirement speech, the strain and the difficulty of stepping away was written all over his face. Nevertheless, Jim delivered his farewell with poise, though choked with emotion at times.

"This is going to be tough," he began, "and I thought saying my wedding vows was tough." Jim laughed as he glanced over at me. In that moment, I thought back to our wedding day and how emotional Jim was when he said his vows. He had indeed struggled to hold back tears during our ceremony, which was shocking. As we stood together now on the Fieldhouse podium before so many fans who loved Jim, it was obvious that leaving the game he loved so passionately was moving him deeply.

"First of all, I want to thank you all for coming," he said. "I have a few words to say to not only my teammates but to all the fans in Buffalo, and to the media, and to everybody who's been not just a Jim Kelly fan but a fan of my family."

I stood next to Jim and tried my best not to look out at the entire Kelly family all lined up in the first row. I knew if I caught their gaze, I would lose it.

"As you might imagine, this hasn't been easy," Jim stated. "I've had to make the most difficult decision of my entire life. I've been playing the game of football for over twenty-eight years. Many of my dreams have been fulfilled, many goals have been achieved, but most important to me, I've been able to take care of the people I love. So today, I stand before you to officially announce my retirement from the Buffalo Bills and the National Football League."

And then Jim stopped, his eyes filling with tears long withheld. Then I started crying. Of course, my being nine months pregnant didn't help.

Jim took a deep breath, pulled himself together, then continued with his speech.

As I glanced out at the hundreds of fans who had come to witness this monumental day for Jim and the Buffalo Bills organization, I was moved. It was such a tribute to Jim and all that he had done for the franchise. He had accomplished so much and given all he had to the team and its dedicated fans—and they knew it.

The tears were many that day, yet our family had much to look forward to. We had retirement plans, which sounded very strange because Jim was still in his thirties and I was just twenty-seven. And in spite of the sense of loss we felt at leaving football, our sorrow and uncertainty were countered by the excitement of expecting our second child, who would be arriving in two short weeks.

I knew exactly what would ease Jim's heartache at giving up the game he loved: telling him that he was about to hold the son he had always wanted. I had made the decision to surprise him and keep it a secret. I couldn't wait to place our baby boy in those strong, battle-scarred hands that had held a football for so long.

With our first baby, Erin Marie, we had found out in advance that we were expecting a girl, but the second time around we had decided to wait—or at least Jim *thought* we had. *Are you kidding me?* I couldn't bear not knowing, so when Jim couldn't make it to one of my routine sonograms, I seized the opportunity to find out for myself. When the doctor told me she saw a little something extra between the baby's legs, I could hardly contain myself. We were going to have the son my husband had longed for!

I'd been hoping for a boy for Jim's sake. He came from a family of six boys and no girls, so you can imagine the pressure. Jim's younger brother Danny was soon to have his first child. Two of Jim's older brothers also had boys, as did Danny's twin, Kevin. So, naturally, the NFL superstar in the family was expected to have a boy, too.

The anticipation was excruciating. I wanted to tell Jim so badly because he was deeply wounded about retiring, and—as tough as he was—the pain of the decision was obvious. Still, to my amazement, I managed to keep quiet those final two weeks.

Then, early in the morning on February 14, 1997—Valentine's Day—my water broke and the contractions began. They intensified during the thirty-minute ride to the hospital, making it seem as though the drive took hours. One thing was on my mind: getting that child out of my dreams and into my arms.

As soon as we walked through the emergency room doors at the hospital, a nurse helped me into the nearest wheelchair, and off we went. I received a routine epidural as my contractions intensified. Thankfully, my labor only lasted a few hours, and even though my focus was on pushing, I was eager to see Jim's reaction once he saw our son.

"It's a boy!" the doctor exclaimed.

Jim's response was priceless: he shouted over and over, "It's a boy! It's a boy!" Although my mind and body were spent, waves of joy filled my heart as I watched Jim erupt with excitement and pride. As family quarterback, Jim was the MVP. He'd remained by my side during the entire delivery, making sure all the right plays were called to address my every need. Jim witnessed the entire birth, cut the umbilical cord, and supervised every move the doctors and nurses made. Now, after a quick kiss on my forehead, he was out the door to grab my parents, who were patiently waiting in the hall. Tears of joy streamed down my face. "Daddy's little *boy* is finally here."

My mom and dad walked into the room, smiling from ear to ear. "I can't believe it's a boy," Mom said as she leaned over to hug me. My dad stood close by and just shook his head, stammering, "Wow." Jim couldn't sit still, so he followed the doctors over to the table where they weighed our son and performed all the newborn baby procedures mothers are usually too wiped out to pay attention to.

After an uneventful pregnancy and fairly easy delivery, the son that Daddy had always dreamed of—the baby destined to be an NFL protégé—finally arrived...a day before his actual due date, yet right on time: on his daddy's thirty-seventh birthday.

No birthday present could compare to the gift of a son. We were amazed and overwhelmed with joy. Our seven-pound, fourteen-ounce dream come true measured twenty-one-and-a half inches long, and I don't mind telling you, he was strikingly handsome.

I let Jim name each of our children. I had picked out plenty of girls' names but boys' names were not as easy to come by. Because of Jim's love for hunting he was determined to name our son Hunter. And so it was, the new rookie was put on the family roster as Hunter James Kelly.

While Hunter was getting acquainted with all the other newborns in the nursery, Jim started working the phones. One of the first people he called was teammate Thurman Thomas, the unstoppable running back who was inducted into the Pro Football Hall of Fame in 2007. Thurman was Jim's go-to guy on the field and also a close personal friend. At first, I thought it was a little odd that Jim would call him before any of his brothers, but his intentions immediately became clear. Thurman and his wife, Patti, had three girls, so being a kid at heart, Jim wanted to rub it in. He was relentless in his quest to rattle Thurman with the good news.

Thurman didn't answer the first time, so Jim left a message. However, boys will be boys, so one call wasn't enough. He placed two more calls, leaving the same message every time: "Oh, did I tell you that I had a son, a boy, born on my birthday? Just in case you didn't hear me the first time, I had a boy, yes, a boy."

Hunter's future was set in stone and the playbook for his life was written. He would play football. He would go hunting. He and his daddy would do all the things that fathers and sons do together. And Jim would be there, guiding Hunter every step of the way. The two would be inseparable. This was going to be a relationship that every boy would long to have with his father: a relationship to behold, to envy, to respect.

It didn't take long for the media to catch wind of the good news and gather at the hospital, hoping to hear firsthand about Team Kelly's new rookie. After Jim was certain that Hunter and I were comfortable, he stepped out to address the curious reporters. With something much more important than football to talk about, he could hardly contain his enthusiasm. It was the birthday he would never forget, for he had been given the most precious gift in the world. Not even a Super Bowl win could compare to this triumph.

Before Jim walked out the door, I smiled at him and said, "Happy birthday." Then I snuggled Hunter close, stared into his eyes, and whispered, "You are a gift."

Finally alone with my son, I explored every inch of his tiny body to make sure everything was okay. The nurse had assured me that Hunter passed all the mandatory newborn screening tests with flying colors, but examining his little body for myself was a must. It's a mom thing. If you've held your own baby after giving birth, then you know.

Fresh out of the womb, Hunter's body looked strong and solid. His facial features were beautiful, with the cutest little nose, perfect lips, and big, bluish-green, almond-shaped eyes that sparkled. His skin was flawless and radiant, and he had such a full head of dark brown hair that he could have made his daddy jealous.

I'll never forget those first few moments alone with my son. Hunter captured my heart immediately, and I just knew he was destined to be extraordinary.

And in those few peaceful moments in the hospital, as I held Hunter...

Everything was perfect.

Chapter 2

Welcome Home

Hunter seemed so content and peaceful; he barely cried or fussed during our two-day hospital stay. It was apparent that he was just happy to finally be out in the world. He must have heard all the exciting things planned for him and could hardly wait to get out in the backyard to toss the football around with his dad.

As for me, after spending two days in the hospital, I couldn't wait to get home and introduce Hunter to his big sister, Erin Marie. Erin was nearly two years old at the time and she was anxious to finally see the baby that had been hiding in Mommy's belly for so long.

Jim and I were not married when Erin Marie was born on May 4, 1995. We had met when Jim was at the top of the most-eligible-bachelor list; wealthy, famous, successful—and living like it. Jim was a notorious partier, and his extravagant postgame parties were the talk of Buffalo. I, in contrast, was twenty-one years old, fresh out of college, full of high expectations, and very naïve. While Jim had been completing passes in the end zone to fill Rich Stadium and take his team to the Super Bowl, I had been studying abroad in London, England, to finish out my final semester of college. I never would have expected the Buffalo Bills or Jim Kelly to be in my future.

But at one of those parties, after a preseason game in September 1991, Jim and I did meet. Some friends of a friend of Jim's invited my friend and me—you know how it works. Jim's parties were only for the "somebodies." You had to know somebody or be personally invited to walk through the door. Otherwise, you wouldn't make it past "Big Ed," who happened to be a close friend of Jim's. At six feet five inches and four hundred–plus pounds, Big Ed stood at the door enforcing the rules of the house. If you weren't invited, you didn't get in.

I will never forget the first night I walked through the doors of Jim Kelly's house. Talk about intimidated. My girlfriend and I felt absurdly out of place, but we were determined to make this night go down in history. And that it did.

Jim's party room was something to see. Even a non–football fan would have appreciated the one-of-a-kind sports and celebrity memorabilia that covered every square inch of wall space. The hallways leading to the bathroom were filled with framed photo memories of Jim and all sorts of famous people, including Michael Jordan, Magic Johnson, Cal Ripken, Donald Trump, Bill Cosby. While a few family pictures were scattered throughout, the majority of Jim's wall of fame consisted of pictures of beautiful women. As I looked at Jim's proud display, I thought to myself, *Who is this guy and what's the big deal?*

Eventually, the highly anticipated introduction was made. It seemed like time stood still when we first met. I was so nervous. My dad would have done anything to meet this guy, and here I was. In the midst of that crowded room filled with famous athletes and beautiful women, Jim took the time to meet me. It was obvious that he had been drinking, and though our conversation was short and sweet, Jim was very gracious and polite. The last thing he said to me in those few moments was, "You have the most beautiful green eyes."

While flattered by the compliment, my mind and heart had already determined not to fall for any one-liners. Throughout the rest of the night, Jim flirted with me while I played hard to get. My friend and I spent a lot of time in the bathroom laughing our heads off at all we were experiencing. We couldn't believe we were actually at Jim Kelly's house and that he was showing interest in me! Yet I didn't want to take any of it too seriously.

Before we left the party that night, Jim asked me for my phone number and, believe it or not, I didn't give it to him. Becoming another notch in his belt was not in my game plan.

At work about a week later I answered the phone and was shocked to hear Jim's voice on the other end. As Jim explained how he'd found out where I worked, I did my best to keep my composure. He ultimately asked me for a date, which I agreed to without hesitation. Jim offered to have his limo driver pick me up, but rather than seem impressed by all the celebrity stuff, I decided to meet him at his home. Even now, I shake my head over that decision. What was I thinking? A gentleman should pick his girl up—it's just the proper thing to do. (Don't forget that, Erin and Camryn!)

I ended up driving to Jim's house from that date forward. Afraid of what my father would think about me spending a night out with the NFL's most eligible bachelor, I asked my mother to keep our first date a secret. She waited until I left the house that evening before spilling the news. It's a good thing, too, because my father understandably had major reservations about the whole thing. My parents watched the clock until my safe return home. And no wonder—I was only twenty-one years old and still under their roof.

That night would be the first of many adjustments my family

would have to make as Jim and I spent more and more time together. Simply put, everything about Jim and his lifestyle was drastically different from what I was accustomed to. For Jim, life was just one big party once the game was over. He was completely focused on football when it was time for football, but he used his free time to enjoy every ounce of his celebrity.

Though clueless about his world, I tried my best to act as if I had it all figured out. Learning to roll with the punches while adjusting to life Kelly-style was my only option. Because Jim was recognized everywhere we went, I had to master the ins and outs of being in public with him: head down, walk fast, and if someone yells out, "Hey, Jim Kelly!"—just keep walking.

Although it could be annoying to have people screaming one's name, I was so impressed with Jim's patience toward his adoring fans. He was always willing to sign an autograph and was particularly kind to kids. Jim's unpretentious way made him very approachable. Despite his national prominence, Jim was just an ordinary guy. Still, it was all so crazy, especially during the Super Bowl days. Everybody wanted a piece of Jim—no one more than me—and we had to constantly adjust our lives around the incessant demands for his attention.

A year and a half after we met, I decided to move out of my parents' home. Bent on personal success and proving myself worthy of adulthood, I dove into the many possibilities available at the time and settled in South Florida, with a career in television marketing and production as my focus.

Even though I was having a blast down in the Sunshine State, the long-distance relationship thing with Jim just wasn't working. In my absence Jim realized that he was willing to give up some things in order to have me by his side, and eventually he asked me to move in with him. We'd been dating for almost three years by this time. It was a huge commitment for Jim. After all, these were the Super Bowl years—the glory days—and he was the Buffalo Bills' marquee quarterback. But it was also a huge commitment for me.

The decision to move back to Western New York and into Jim's home would ultimately alter the rest of my life, and Jim's as well. On May 4, 1994, exactly one year prior to the birth of our first child, I crossed the threshold of his house and simultaneously set off a domino effect of events that would completely transform my world.

Four months after Jim's bachelor pad became my new address, my period was late. My menstrual cycle had never been consistent, so no alarms went off at first. However, once two weeks had passed and my period still had not started, I grew very concerned.

Jim was wrapped up with football; I didn't want to bother him. But I did need to know if I was pregnant, so I decided to purchase a home pregnancy test. The entire scenario was so foreign to me that I didn't realize how many different versions of tests were available. Even if I had known, I felt so embarrassed that the last thing I would have wanted to do was linger in a store and compare brands.

I hurriedly purchased the cheapest test and called my close friend Mary and asked her if I could stop over. Little did she know that my plan was to take the pregnancy test in her home. I didn't want to be alone.

Many thoughts surged through my already-cluttered mind: *What if I'm pregnant? Everyone will know. How will I tell my parents? What have I done? I should have never moved into that house.* I was terrified.

Once I took the test, I handed Mary the stick. "What does this mean?" I asked. Her eyes widened and she looked at me with a smile. "Well, it looks like that's a solid line right there, so…"

"Does that mean I'm pregnant?" I interrupted. Then, panicked, I rationalized: "But you touched it, so maybe it's wrong. Maybe I didn't follow the directions properly. I think I should go buy another test—a better one—and do it again. What do you think?"

We laughed off the initial test—figuring I'd gotten what I'd paid for—but I was starting to worry. *Surely the positive reading was a mistake, right?* The best thing to do was to head to the nearest store and purchase the most expensive pregnancy test available. And that's exactly what I did.

The second test read positive as well.

Mary took one look at the stick and walked toward me with arms outstretched. "Jill, what are you going to do?" she whispered as she hugged me close.

"I have to call my mom," I replied. "She's in Chicago, but I can't wait until she gets back. I have to call her today. Like right now."

This predicament seemed unimaginable, even though my own actions had brought me to this point. A rush of reality slammed into my so-called perfect world as Mary and I sat together and wept.

When we walked outside and over to my truck, Mary tried to encourage me. "Jill, whatever you need, I'm here for you. Give me a call after you talk to your mom, okay?"

We hugged one more time and then I drove away. I was a fearful mess, pondering all sorts of scenarios in my head. *Now what? How am I going to tell my parents? How am I going to tell Jim? What will he say? What if he wants me to get an abortion? That is not an option.*

I was absolutely overwhelmed. Jim's bachelor pad wasn't ready for a baby. But more importantly, neither were Jim and I.

My mother was away on business, but the phone call had to be made. When she got on the line, I nervously blurted out the news: "Mom, I'm sorry for calling you while you're traveling but I need to talk to you. . . . Mom, I'm pregnant."

"Are you sure?" she asked. "How do you know?" Then, "Oh my, Jill, I can't believe you're telling me this over the phone. I'll try and get the next flight out of Chicago. And don't worry, everything's going to be okay. I'll be home as soon as I can get there."

I can only imagine what was going through my mother's mind as I shared the details of my afternoon at Mary's house. "Mom, what am I going to do?" I asked. "I'm scared to tell Dad; he's going to freak out. How am I going to tell Jim?"

Thankfully, my mom was able to cancel her meetings and take the next flight out of Chicago. As soon as she got into town, my mother, who was and is my best friend, met me at a restaurant, where we spent the majority of our time together in tears. We decided that she would be the one to tell my father and brother. The one thing I remember my mother saying was, "We will be here for you no matter what, Jill."

While comforted and encouraged by her words, I was also terribly ashamed. Afraid of how my father would react, I couldn't help but wonder, *Will he still love me? Will he support me no matter what?*

What a mess.

My brother, Jack, has since told me that both he and Dad were understandably shocked at the news. Initially, my father was angry and fearful. He felt helpless and wanted to make sure Jim would do the right thing. He certainly didn't want his daughter to be abandoned by some flamboyant football star.

Fortunately, as vulnerable and concerned as my parents felt, they were determined to support me through thick and thin. In the meantime, I was grappling with perhaps the most frightening questions of all: How in the world would I tell Jim? *When* should I tell him?

He had an important game coming up, and I didn't want to break the news before then. The distraction could ruin his concentration and negatively affect his play, I reasoned. If the team lost, he might blame it all on me. Then where would that leave us?

While I tried to figure out the best approach and timing with Jim, there was one thing I clearly needed to do: confirm the pregnancy officially. I had a blood test done, and on September 21, the results came back—positive. The secret couldn't wait any longer. Jim needed to know.

The following afternoon, after a long day of practice and reviewing game films, Jim walked wearily into the house. I met him at the door and told him we needed to talk. Intimate communication was a challenge for us at the time. Jim was a bottom-line guy, a vigilant, hard-core leader who wanted everything simple and to the point. My way, on the other hand, was to elaborate and talk things through... thoroughly. We walked back to our bedroom, where I took a seat in his favorite recliner. He sat on the couch nearby.

Initially I held it together while we talked about the day's events. But as soon as I started to tell him about missing my period, I fell apart. The words wouldn't come out.

Jim was shaken but unusually calm. "Are you sure?" he asked hesitantly.

Nervously, I struggled through the details, even telling him about my pregnancy test experience at Mary's, which ended up providing a much-needed moment of comic relief for us. The fleeting laughter was welcomed with open arms, and suddenly so was I.

Jim couldn't have been more loving. He gathered me in his embrace, assuring me that everything was going to be okay. "Jill, you know I love kids, and you know I love you. We're just going to have children sooner than I expected, that's all. It will all work out. I know it will. So don't worry, and please stop crying. We're going to be fine."

Always the optimist, Jim talked about doing the "right thing" and getting married before the child was born. We also discussed how he would tell his parents and five brothers, and how we would handle the media frenzy once the word got out. Although I knew Jim was stunned, he was very tender and honorable. And yet in spite of his confident, calm exterior, inwardly he was afraid, too.

I was probably most concerned about how Jim's mother, Alice, would respond. She had raised six rough-and-tumble boys, and she deserved every bit of the respect she commanded. As the grand matriarch of the Kelly clan, if she didn't like you—you were history.

Jim had gotten his mother's approval to continue dating me, but now what? She hadn't been crazy about our living together to begin with, and now I was carrying her son's child! Would this woman, who didn't allow Jim and me to sleep in the same room whenever she was around, blame me? She'd made it very clear that the marital bed was to be respected. *What if Jim's entire family shuns me?* I thought. *What if they convince Jim to leave me and I'm forced to become a single mother? What am I going to do?*

I wasn't present when Jim told his mom and dad that we were pregnant, and their disappointed response, while expected, made me feel all the more awkward and alienated. However, after the initial shock of it wore off, life went on as usual. At least it seemed to for everyone but me.

Eventually the focus drifted back to winning football games, with Jim's family assuming their game-day demeanor: food, football, and fun. Despite the difficult circumstances, I remember those days fondly. Jim's family looked forward to every home game, and so did I.

In fact, every time the Buffalo Bills took the field at Rich

Stadium/Ralph Wilson Stadium, the entire Kelly family suited up for a weekend of memories. Win or lose, they were ready to party. Everyone had a role to play, and what appeared to be complete chaos was actually a well-organized and structured game-day routine. In fact, game day was more like a production.

Tailgating and pregame warm-up festivities began as soon as the Kelly boys flew into town. Jim's aunt Toni from Pittsburgh would prepare the secret pregame spaghetti sauce on Saturday while friends and family huddled around the basement party room at Kelly's Irish Pub.

While Jim was at the hotel mentally preparing, the rest of the family and countless friends prepared our house for the much-anticipated pre- and postgame action. Jim's dad, Joe, and his five brothers—Pat, Ed, Ray, Danny, and Kevin—readied the motor home for Kelly-style tailgating, while the sisters-in-law dressed the children in number 12 jerseys.

Jim's close friend and housemate, Tommy Good, was always the guy in charge. He was the keeper of game tickets and everything else important, so of course everybody wanted to please Tommy. As Jim's trusted confidant, "T-Good," as we called him, protected all that concerned the Kelly family. Knowing I had earned Alice Kelly's respect and approval, I was determined to get to know this guy. And I did. Our many confrontations and shared celebrations eventually produced such a friendship and trust that Tommy is our firstborn's, Erin Marie's, godfather—an honor he takes very seriously.

While T-Good dished out the best seats in the stadium, the rest of the Kelly clan focused on cold Crown Royal shots, Coors Light, spicy tailgate chili, and redneck fun. Our tailgates were the envy of Bills fans. Everyone knew where to find the Kelly motor home, but Big Ed made sure most folks kept their distance.

One Bills Drive was, and in a way still is, our second home.

Chapter 3

Mr. and Mrs. Quarterback

As my relationship with Jim grew, my life gradually became all about football. Or should I say, all about Jim Kelly. Though I was still in my early twenties, my identity was being swallowed up in what appeared to be every woman's dream. I was no longer Jill Waggoner but the girlfriend of Jim Kelly, All-Pro quarterback for the Buffalo Bills.

Then on November 2, 1994, my situation shifted drastically yet again.

"Will you marry me?"

It was a magical moment filled with emotion. After months of wondering and waiting, Jim finally proposed. There was nothing unusual about that evening at Ilio DiPaolo's restaurant, not initially anyway. The owner, Dennis, a dear friend of the Kelly family, sat us in the back of his Italian bistro in our favorite private room—the Buffalo Room. Decorated with all sorts of Bills memorabilia and very isolated, it was the perfect spot for Jim to pop the long-awaited question.

We ordered the usual that evening—the Abruzzi Platter for Jim and Chicken Abruzzi for me. When it came time for dessert, which I happen to love, Jim told me that Dennis had prepared something extra-special for us. Still oblivious to what Jim had planned, I agreed to try the dessert surprise. Little did I know that dessert that evening would come with a three-carat-diamond engagement ring!

As Jim asked me to close my eyes, I never dreamed that when I opened them again my world would change forever. While I sat there waiting in the corner of the Buffalo Room, Dennis and our photographer, Danny—whom Jim had brought in to make sure we would have tangible memories of this special evening—scurried quietly behind the scenes to ensure the moment would be perfect.

"Open your eyes," Jim said.

I did, and in front of me on the table was a beautiful heart-shaped cake with a sparkling diamond ring placed in the center. Inscribed on the cake were the words, "Will you marry me?"

Completely overwhelmed, I blinked back tears amid the flash of cameras.

I was speechless.

"Well, will you?" Jim asked nervously.

I just looked at him as he dropped to his knees, grabbed my hands, and asked again, "Will you marry me, Jill?"

As Jim reached for the engagement ring, I whispered, "Yes, yes, yes, I will." Jim wiped the frosting off the most beautiful ring I had ever laid eyes on and gently slipped the shimmering symbol of our love on my finger, then hugged me like never before.

I was surprised and relieved, but also scared. In the midst of the most amazing proposal a woman could hope for, fear and doubt cast a shadow across my heart. A shadow that had probably first arisen on that September night years before at Jim's party when I'd seen the many photos of women on Jim's wall. As happy as I was, part of me wondered—*Does Jim really love me? Do I love him? Is this for real? Will this love go the distance and endure until death do us part? Is he marrying me because I'm carrying his firstborn child?* I wanted so badly to be certain and longed for assurance. Unfortunately, these questions would linger uneasily in my heart and mind for years to come.

Jim and I had discussed getting married before Erin Marie was born, but we also envisioned a grand wedding fit for a Super Bowl quarterback and his one-and-only cheerleader. (Contrary to rumor, I had never been a Buffalo Jill—the official name of the Bills' cheerleaders—I think my name consistently caused that confusion.) After talking it through, Jim and I opted to wait so we could savor every aspect of planning the event of our lifetime.

As tough and manly as Jim is, he was very much involved in the details of our wedding. From our engagement to our fairy-tale honeymoon in Italy, Jim was into it. We spent many nights mulling over all sorts of ceremony specifics: Where would we get married? What type of entertainment and food should we have? Is there a venue big enough to accommodate over nine hundred guests? Eventually we realized we were in way over our heads, so we hired a wedding planner.

At this point in our life, money was no object, so everything had to be top-notch. My search for the perfect wedding dress began in Buffalo. Believe it or not, I ended up purchasing the first dress I tried on. However, in order to exhaust all my options, my girlfriends and I made a weekend trip to New York City, hitting the top couture wedding salons.

We set out to find the most beautiful gown, only to discover that the higher-end shops wouldn't take us seriously. It reminded me of the scene in the movie *Pretty Woman*, where the sales-people in exclusive retail stores snub Julia Roberts because she doesn't appear to be their class of client. Unfortunately for their gross profit that day, the stores we visited in New York City weren't gracious enough to learn that I was a Super Bowl quarterback's fiancée!

Regardless of the treatment we received, our trip to the city was a blast. Perhaps it was just as well that we didn't find a dress that weekend. The designer gown I selected was featured in the February 10, 1997, issue of *People* magazine as one of the ten best wedding dresses of the year. The late Carolyn Bessette (John F. Kennedy Jr.'s wife) and top fashion model Christie Brinkley were also part of the top ten—not bad company for a twenty-six-year-old from Western New York.

The gown, elaborately hand-made by Italian designer Pino Lanchetti, consisted of three separate pieces of Italian silk, tulle, and lace; a strapless silk crepe sheath; and a long-sleeved, white lace overlay complete with sixty-seven individual buttons down the back and a detachable silk tulle overskirt. My fairy-tale princess dress was a bear to get on and off, so it's a good thing I had plenty of bridesmaids to assist me on my wedding day.

Our wedding party was huge, consisting of twenty-six people that included close friends from high school and college as well as family and some of Jim's teammates. Jim's younger brother Danny was the best man, and my best friend from Notre Dame High School, Karyn, was the maid of honor. Except for my cousin Jessica, a born-again Christian at the time, our group was a bunch of hard-core partiers.

The fun began as soon as gifts started arriving, right after we sent out wedding invitations. Jim and I had registered locally for the usual—china, crystal, and other impractical household clutter. So we were truly surprised when a huge wooden pallet loaded with toilet paper arrived. It was completely intended as a joke, but it ended up being the most talked-about and useful—if unusual—gift of all. Finding storage space for that much toilet paper was not easy, and I'm sure our neighbors thought we had serious bathroom issues. Incredibly, we used our last roll almost a year to the day of our wedding. Imagine that.

Come May 18, 1996—our wedding day—hundreds of onlookers lined the boulevard entrance of St. Christopher's Roman Catholic Church outside Buffalo while eager paparazzi packed designated areas, awaiting our arrival. Like most weddings do, the day flew by. As John Barry's beautiful song "Somewhere in Time" drifted throughout the enormous sanctuary, I linked arms with my father, and he looked at me and whispered, "Are you ready?"

With a nervous smile and a nod of the head, I hugged him. Then off we headed, down the aisle. Cameras flashed all around us as we slowly made our way to the front of the sanctuary. It was all so perfect.

After Jim hugged my dad, he took my hand and escorted me up the altar steps. Reverend Philip Oriole, a close friend from Pennsylvania, and Monsignor Francis Weldgen, chaplain for the Buffalo Bills, cracked a few jokes to kick off the ceremony.

"Buffalo has been waiting a long time for two things," Father Fran said. "To win a Super Bowl, and for Jim to get married." We all laughed.

Jim appeared very calm—not to mention very handsome in his double-breasted, traditional black tuxedo. I, on the other hand, was a nervous wreck. I think part of me was still in shock that I was actually getting married! *This is a big deal! A really big deal!* I thought to myself. But even on this momentous day, doubt tried to overshadow me: *What in the world am I doing here? Who do I think I am, marrying an NFL quarterback?*

We had a traditional Catholic wedding ceremony, complete with Gospel readings, the lighting of the unity candle, recitation of the Lord's Prayer, and the taking of Communion. I tried desperately to take it all in, but the entire day is more a collage of defining moments than detailed memories.

What I remember most vividly about the ceremony is really what made the day unforgettable: Jim choked up when he said his vows. Jim's not one for showing his emotions, so when he had trouble maintaining his composure, I was shocked and humbled. *Could it be that Jim actually means what he's saying—in good times and bad, till death do us part? Do I mean it?*

After the bridal kiss and our presentation as Mr. and Mrs. Jim Kelly, we made our way to the city of Buffalo's breathtaking waterfront and lighthouse for pictures. Believe it or not, we had so much fun that both photographers neglected to take a single photo of my mother and me together—go figure. Maybe they were having a little too much fun. In any case, after the pictures we headed to the New York State Armory for the much-anticipated reception. The site was an old military storage base being used by a local unit of the New York National Guard. The historic landmark, located on Connecticut Street in the heart of Buffalo, looks like a small castle. It was the only local facility available that could accommodate the number of guests we had.

For security purposes and to protect our privacy, guests were required to present a numbered invitation to enter the reception. The rustic old building was flanked with security and media as the wedding-goers filed through the front doors. Meanwhile, Jim and I snuck in through a private entrance.

All the pomp, pretense, and splendor of the entire event made me laugh. You would've thought we were the prince and princess of Buffalo. At that time, oddly, I guess we were.

The Armory had been transformed into a splendid alabaster sanctuary. Tables and chairs were dressed in crisp white linen, and an elegant floral centerpiece accented each table. The aroma from hundreds of flowers infused the entire building. A beautiful archway display of fresh white roses and twinkling lights greeted each guest as they entered the cathedral-like main room. Everywhere you looked, the room seemed to dance and sparkle.

In the midst of ice sculptures, mounds of fresh shrimp and raw seafood, butler-passed hors d'oeuvres, carving stations, and many mouth-watering delicacies, our wedding cake stole the show. Jim had been determined to design our cake. So much so that he spent time drawing exactly how he envisioned it should look. With the help of Carolyn—a very sweet and patient pastry artist—our dream cake became a reality.

The incredible dessert, made for an army (or a football team), stood more than seven feet tall and weighed over five hundred pounds. Each of the nine tiers was a different flavor of cake, including white, chocolate, various cheesecakes, and even carrot. Its smooth fondant surface featured sugar vases filled with cascading roses and other flowers made of frosting.

I don't know how Carolyn got our cake from her bakery to the wedding reception, but she did. Unfortunately, the only taste I got was the portion Jim shoved into my mouth after we did the traditional cutting of the wedding cake. Even smeared all over my face, it was luscious, and yes, Jim's face was covered with cake, too.

For me, the public attention our ceremony and reception received paled in comparison to the beauty and wonder of it all. Our wedding day truly was perfect...except for one thing. Jim's mother, Alice, had passed away barely a month before our wedding celebration.

Mrs. Kelly fought a very long, cruel battle with emphysema, and the entire family was at her side the moment she took her last breath. In her honor, Jim danced with our one-year-old daughter, Erin, to his mother's favorite song, "Memories (The Way We Were)" by Barbra Streisand. The beauty of the moment helped ease the sting of our loss, but Alice Kelly was dearly missed.

After a two-week, whirlwind honeymoon in Italy, we couldn't wait to get home to Erin Marie. Fourteen days is a long time to be absent when your baby is growing so rapidly. My parents made sure Erin got the royal treatment while we were away. "Gramma-razzi" (like *paparazzi*, a humorous nickname we christened my mother with because of her obsession for taking pictures) conducted many photo sessions of "Princess Kelly" decked out in all sorts of adorable outfits.

As you'd expect, everything Erin did was incredible in our eyes, and like most new parents, we were overly enthusiastic whenever our firstborn attempted anything. She was always the star of the show and demanded our undivided attention—which we were happy to give. Once all the wedding excitement was over, our new normal as a family began: Jim resumed his hectic workout and travel schedule, and Erin and I hung out the rest of the summer. Daddy wasn't home that much, so the two of us did a lot of girlie activities together.

I went into marriage full of starry-eyed expectations and consequently found myself disappointed in Jim and our relationship more often than not. I had known what I was getting myself into as far as the overall lifestyle of an NFL star, but I was hoping that somehow our marriage would change things. Now that we were actually newlyweds, I imagined that Jim would *want* to spend more time at home with Erin and me. Unfortunately, that was just wishful thinking, and Jim spent most of that first summer of our marriage traveling. I often wondered where he was and tried to stay on top of his ever-changing schedule, but it wasn't easy.

One of the responsibilities I appointed myself that summer was to clean house. Not just the usual vacuuming and dusting, but giving our home a major overhaul. As part of that task, I was determined to get rid of the remnants of Jim's bachelor life. I descended on drawers full of letters, cards, female garments that didn't belong to me, as well as pictures of pretty girls—some with clothes on and some without. Some of the items I discovered were shocking. In fact, I remember thinking to myself... *And this is someone's daughter. What a shame.*

How awkward I felt. I wanted to make our house a home. A normal home. A secure and special place for our daughter to grow up. Yet it was becoming apparent that there would be nothing normal about being married to Jim Kelly.

As I sorted through drawers and closets full of stuff, I found myself growing increasingly angry with Jim. His past, and the baggage that went along with it, was everywhere. My relationship baggage was history; I had just assumed Jim's would be, too.

If anyone should be purging the past, I reasoned, it should be him. But he wasn't the one sifting through this stuff. It was me, his wife. Not even three months into our marriage, I was the one spending afternoons cleaning skeletons from my husband's closet.

Skeletons that he should have handled before the wedding.

Skeletons that filled my mind and heart with jealousy, fear, doubt, and mistrust, simply because they were still there.

What a great start to an already-fragile relationship, I thought to myself.

The leftovers from his bachelorhood, coupled with my unfulfilled expectations, slowly began to harden my heart, and the shadow over our relationship darkened. I grew so bitter and defensive that every time Jim walked through the door, I allowed my ever-growing negativity toward him to take over.

Then, once again, it happened: my period was late. This time I knew exactly what to do and was very excited to discover the results—positive. The timing was uncanny. After calculating the days, the doctor determined that the baby was conceived during our honeymoon. What perfect timing.

Maybe this child would be the one to draw Jim back home, away from all the distractions and temptations he was so caught up in. I could only hope.

Erin watched my belly grow as nine months flew by, unaware that she was about to have a baby brother. (In my defense, if I was going to keep it a secret from her dad, she certainly couldn't know either!) I had lots of fun preparing for our son to arrive. Granted, I had to be covert about everything, but buying all sorts of baby boy clothes and toys was a blast. Hiding them, on the other hand, was a challenge.

Fortunately, my little surprise remained a surprise until that day in February 1997 when Hunter James Kelly was born. Jim's birthday and Valentine's Day would never be the same. Little did we know how drastically our lives would soon be changed as well.

Chapter 4

Broken

I'd like for you and Jim to come into my office so we can discuss Hunter's test results. Can you come on Monday?" Dr. Duffner asked in a monotone voice.

"Yes. What time and where?"

Our conversation was so short and to the point that it didn't even dawn on me to ask her the results over the phone. Then, when the phone hit the receiver, it hit me. If Hunter's blood tests were normal, Dr. Duffner would have said so.

But wait. Hunter had passed all the newborn tests with flying colors. God had given us a beautiful, healthy son. So what was going on?

The first month of Hunter's life, he appeared to be a normal, healthy baby except for showing some signs of colic. The second month, he became more irritable; and by the end of the third month, he was spending most of his waking hours screaming. Our pediatrician continued to believe it was colic, so we tried practically every formula and bottle on the market. When Hunter became even more irritable—stiffening his arms and legs, and failing to achieve any developmental milestones—the doctor said he was showing signs of cerebral palsy. We were devastated but determined to do everything we could to give Hunter the best life possible.

In Hunter's fourth month, his body became more rigid. He was having trouble swallowing, and he started experiencing mild seizures. Because Hunter's health continued to decline, our pediatrician suggested he go to a child neurologist. Hunter's neurologist, Dr. Duffner, decided to test his blood. Now she was asking us to come to her office to discuss the results.

"Something's wrong," Jim said after I shared the phone conversation with him. "If it were good news, she would've told you over the phone. This isn't going to be good."

My mom stayed at the house with Erin and Hunter while Jim and I made the trip to Children's Hospital that Monday morning. The beauty of that summer day was clouded by the gut-wrenching feeling that Jim and I both had. Lost in our individual thoughts, we said nothing to each other as we traveled into the city.

When we arrived at Dr. Duffner's office, Jim's brother Danny was waiting at the entrance to walk in with us. We were greeted and escorted into a dim room where Dr. Duffner and our pediatrician stood. *Why is our pediatrician here? That's not a good sign,* I thought to myself.

As we exchanged hellos, it was obvious that something was dreadfully wrong. Looking around at all the sullen faces told the whole story. These were doctors—professionals—but they could not hide their feelings. I sensed an overwhelming heaviness in our midst. My heart felt as though it were beating outside my shirt, and my hands were drenched with sweat.

The small room we were in had no windows. A table was squeezed in amid shelves of old textbooks, leaving barely enough room for any of us to sit. The room was damp and smelled very musty and old. It was such a nondescript and lifeless place that it was easy to imagine no one ever got good news here.

Once we were seated Dr. Duffner explained what type of blood tests she took and exactly what she was looking for. She then proceeded to detail where Hunter's blood work was sent, who tested it, and why. It was all very foreign to us.

Just tell us! Just tell us! I thought. *What's wrong with Hunter? What's hurting him?*

Finally, she said, "Your son has been diagnosed with a fatal genetic disease called Krabbe Leukodystrophy. There is no treatment for this disease and no cure. The average life expectancy for babies diagnosed with infantile Krabbe is fourteen months. Hunter will probably not live to see his second birthday. We can help you make your son more comfortable but—"

I had to interrupt. "What do you mean, there's no treatment? There's got to be *something* we can do—somewhere we can take him." The thought of there being no help for our son—for *Jim Kelly's* son—was unfathomable.

"There is nowhere to take your son because there is no one working on this disease," Dr. Duffner explained. "He will need to get a feeding tube as soon as possible in order to eat, if that's what you choose to do."

Her words felt like daggers penetrating my heart, and they kept coming, one right after another. *A feeding tube? What's that and why? . . . What does she mean, if we choose to? We'll do whatever it takes for Hunter. He needs to eat; we can't just let him starve to death. . . . What is she trying to say?* My mind was on overload, racing with questions, full of fear and confusion.

Dr. Duffner reiterated, "No one is doing anything for this disease. It is rare, and very few people know anything about it. Dr. David Wenger, a doctor in Philadelphia, assured me that nothing is being done anywhere. If you'll excuse me...." She got up and walked to a desk in an adjacent room.

Though I was completely numb, I watched Dr. Duffner's every move as she proceeded to pick up a phone and make a call. I couldn't hear what she was saying, but I was very attentive to her facial expressions, gestures, and body language—it wasn't good news.

After she hung up, she returned to the table, sat down, and explained, "That was Dr. Hugo Moser from the Kennedy Krieger Institute," she explained. "He is a world-renowned doctor working on ALD–adrenoleukodystrophy—a different type of leukodystrophy. I wanted to ask him if he knew of anyone doing any type of treatment, even experimentally. He said no."

She paused, then continued: "I'm so sorry. I will do everything I can to help your son. But the disease has already progressed so fast that I don't think he will live much longer."

As my mind tried desperately to process all the horrific news that had just been dropped into our lives, my body felt weak and lifeless. Tears started streaming down my cheeks and my head was throbbing. I sank into my chair as if I weighed a thousand pounds. It was hard to catch my breath; I felt as if my very life was being choked out of me.

This can't be happening. Not to us—not to Hunter....

Jim remained very calm, not shedding even a single tear. I suppose he was trying to be strong for my sake.

Before we left the neurology office, Dr. Duffner gave us some additional information, and then we scheduled a preliminary appointment for Hunter's feeding-tube surgery.

The ride home was horrible. The frustration and fear of the unknown weighed so heavily on my heart that I just wanted to run away and be by myself. Desperation like I'd never imagined swept through my body and bombarded my mind with over-whelming dread. *What are we going to do?* I thought as I stared out the passenger window. *Isn't there someone out there who can help us? My amazing, beautiful son is dying. This can't be happening. It can't be true.*

Life all around us continued to rush by as we drove home that morning, helpless and hopeless. People were hurrying to and from work, visiting each other, laughing over lunch. They were going about their normal day, while our lives had just been turned completely upside down.

I wanted to scream, "This isn't fair! Could all of you just stop for one minute and everything stand still?"—because all I knew as life had come to a screeching halt.

Jim stayed quiet. What could he say or do? He was just as confused and frightened as I was.

In Jim's Own Words

I was numb and shocked. I didn't want to believe it was true. I didn't know what to do. It just didn't seem real. Hunter looked good; except for all the crying, he seemed healthy. There was no history of disease in my family or in Jill's, so where did something like this come from?

At first I was ticked off at everything and everybody—especially God. Why did my son, born on my birthday, have to be sick? And not just sick. He was dying, and there was nothing I could do to help him. Nothing. How are you supposed to just take your son home and watch him deteriorate? Watch him die? I wanted to do something, anything. But what?

We're Kellys—we don't give up. We don't ever give up. . . . I wasn't going to let Hunter go without a fight. . . . He's my son, my only son. . . . But there was absolutely nothing I could do to make him better.

—————

When Jim and I returned home from the doctor's office, my mother was waiting for us. I gave her the details of the test results.

"There must be a mistake," she proclaimed with confidence. "I don't believe it. There has to be something we can do. I want to talk to the doctor myself."

As my mother went to call Dr. Duffner, I sat on the couch with Hunter and wept. Erin was very confused. "What's wrong, Mommy? Why are you crying?"

How do you explain the unexplainable to a two-year-old? How do you tell a child that her brother is going to die? Is there a way to communicate pain that you can't comprehend yourself?

As I sat drenched in tears, cradling Hunter in my arms, Erin snuggled up next to me and whispered, "Everything's going to be okay, Mommy. Everything's going to be okay."

Little did she know that everything was not going to be okay. Our lives would never be the same.

Chapter 5

Searching for Hope

When Jim and I were told that our son would not live to see his second birthday, my quest for hope began. I was on a desperate search for treatment and a cure, aching for even a shred of hope and some sign of the God I thought I knew growing up.

Our family had plunged into a wilderness of despair that every parent fears. I was convinced help was out there, but where? Who could rescue us and give us some hope to cling to?

Though he might have wanted to, it was pretty obvious that Jim couldn't save the day for me or our family. If anything, Hunter's diagnosis only made the problems in our marriage and family all the more evident.

After Jim retired from the NFL and Hunter got sick, I assumed Jim would be around more. His work as a color analyst for NBC (and later, ESPN) necessitated a lot of travel. Still, I thought he would make a way to be with us as much as possible. When he didn't, my resentment grew and bitterness wrapped its vicious, unrelenting coils around my heart. Every time Jim would come home, those coils would tighten, paralyzing what little love and respect I had left. (No wonder the divorce rate is so high for professional athletes, let alone professional athletes with a terminally ill child. The deck was stacked against us big-time.)

With Hunterboy not expected to live very long, we knew this meant his needs would intensify as his illness progressed. Though I wasn't very optimistic that Jim would drop everything to be by his side, I continued to hope that he would. All the while, I was consumed with caring for Hunter. Emotionally and physically I felt drained with nothing left to give. What little energy I had in reserve was spent on Hunter's older sister, Erin. There was no time for Jim. And to be frank, I didn't care. The seed of resentment was well rooted in our marriage by this point, so any desire to respond to him as a wife was gone.

It didn't matter to me that Jim needed to go to this appearance or that event, or that our relationship was in serious trouble; at this point in our lives, all that mattered was our family. We'd been told that our son would probably not live to see his second birthday, and I wanted to spend every minute with him. Why didn't Jim feel the same way? I needed him desperately. I needed him to help me. Hunter and Erin needed their daddy. Hunter especially deserved to have his dad there, and I was furious that Jim wasn't around.

More fire was added to the negativity I already felt toward Jim, and without even realizing it, I grew to despise him.

Our relationship had already taken such a hit before Hunter was even born, and our communication skills were lacking from the beginning, so you can imagine how they deteriorated as time went on. We didn't have much to talk about, ever. Jim's life was drastically different from mine. I was focused on what medicine or treatment Hunter needed, while things that just didn't seem to matter constantly distracted Jim.

We were heading in opposite directions, drifting farther and farther from any semblance of a relationship. Eventually, I didn't care how often Jim was gone or when he was coming home. In fact, I ran such a tight ship that he just messed everything up when he was home anyway. He was out of sight, out of mind as far as I was concerned, and his absence only made my heart grow harder rather than fonder.

To complicate matters even more, we didn't share the same bed because Hunter's medical needs necessitated that someone sleep with him. For the most part, that responsibility became mine, but I occasionally took turns with my mother (and we had a night nurse for a little while, too). But even on those nights when I wasn't taking care of Hunter, I slept alone, away from Jim. The farther away I got from him, literally and figuratively, the more isolated I felt. Help surrounded me—parents, friends, nurses, therapists—and yet the only help I desperately wanted and needed was Jim's. Even when Jim gave his best efforts, though, they just never seemed good enough.

I didn't like the way I was treating Jim, and yet I was just so angry that I didn't know how to act or feel. There was so much confusion and pain in my mind and heart. I wanted Jim to take care of me. I needed him to hold me and tell me that everything was going to be okay, even though we both knew it wouldn't be. There's no shame in saying, I needed my man! We had made this beautiful child together, and the longing to share in this journey with my son's father was excruciatingly intense.

Jim did spend time with Hunter, but I wanted him to walk in my shoes for just one hour and *really* take care of Hunter—to know him as intimately as I did and spend the kind of quality time with him that caring for his physical needs demanded. Of course, I knew that when Jim was with Hunter, he loved it. And HB loved every minute with his dad—especially when they got to watch football together. It was just that I was so wrapped up in my own pain, I couldn't see that Jim had deep pain of his own. Eventually I think he got to the point where he didn't even want to try anymore; it was just too hard to please me. I was looking for him to fill a void in my life and Hunter's that he simply could not fill. And while my expectations of Jim felt reasonable to me at the time, I now realize how unrealistic they really were.

Not only was Jim incapable of filling the abyss my heart was quickly becoming, I would eventually learn that he was never meant to fill it in the first place.

He and I would need to search beyond each other to find the hope we desperately craved. We would need to find a love that would fill our unmet expectations and conquer our fears. And when we did, it would end up saving our marriage and our love.

———

As a young girl, I sat in a creaky old pew every Sunday in the back of St. Vincent's Church on East Avenue. Tucked into the little prison town of Attica, New York, it was a beautiful, modest white church right down the street from my Catholic elementary school. This is the church where I was baptized as an infant and where I had my first Communion and Confirmation. It was the church where I grew up, and where my parents and grandparents grew up as well. As a young girl, it was the church where I imagined getting married someday. In fact, during mass, when I was supposed to be reciting the responsorial psalm, I would often daydream about how the pews would be decorated.

The Stations of the Cross were on the walls in between breathtaking stained-glass windows. Whenever I looked up at them, which wasn't often, the words that came to mind were "Crucify Him! Crucify Him!" I hated shouting those words when we did the Stations before Easter every year. A shiny statue of Mary, the mother of Jesus, was located to the right of the altar near the side entrance of the church. She looked so beautiful and gentle. I can't remember what the statue to the left of the altar looked like, but I remember the cross that hung above the altar. It was massive, and I didn't want to look at it because it made me sad. Jesus' face was heartrending and His body was naked except for the loincloth around His waist. He looked horrible.

I never understood the cross or why Jesus was nailed there to die. And we never talked about Him. Never. The Bible stories taught during Sunday school classes were fun, but I didn't learn anything about Jesus or His sacrifice—the crux of which would've been crucial for me to comprehend if I was ever to have a relationship with Him. I don't remember praying to Him either, but I prayed to Mary a lot. I liked her. I didn't know anything about Mary except that she was the mother of Jesus and she was good. So as I was taught to do from the time I was a little girl, I prayed the Hail Mary: "Hail Mary, full of grace, the Lord is with thee. Blessed are thou among women and blessed is the fruit of thy womb, Jesus. Holy Mary, Mother of God, pray for us sinners, now and at the hour of our death. Amen."

I didn't understand what sin was either, or that I was a sinner...but I prayed about that, too—when I had to. Especially after confession. I couldn't wait to get out of that musty, gloomy cubicle so that I could finish my ten Our Fathers and ten Hail Marys and be on my way.

I was always scared to go behind the curtain into that little confessional booth. You had to whisper so that the other people waiting to go in after you wouldn't hear all your sins. And even worse, I was worried that the priest on the other side of the dense screen might figure out who I was and tell my parents!

What was a kid to do? I tried to sound as unlike me as I could. "Bless me, Father, for I have sinned. My last confession was..."

Unfortunately, I could never remember when my last confession was, so on top of all the other sins I confessed, I had to acknowledge that I'd lied about the date of my last confession.

I thought I was a good girl most of the time anyway, so during a few confessions I even made up some of my sins. I had to say something! It was all so stressful.

As much as I dreaded confession, though, church itself was just a part of life. Going to church was what we did. It didn't matter if my brother, Jack, and I were tired or sick, we had to go. Every Sunday. And we had to look good.

We had our church clothes, our school clothes, and our play clothes. We dressed especially nice on Easter and Christmas. I wasn't much for dresses and skirts, but getting decked out for Easter mass was a must every year. However, as soon as I got home, those clothes were instantly replaced with play clothes. After all, I had to be in something more comfortable before digging through my Easter basket full of goodies.

For me, Easter was about finding where my mother hid my basket of candy. Even as an adult, I seldom thought about the death of Jesus or the historical reality of His glorious resurrection. But after Hunter got sick, my search for God intensified as if my very life, and Hunter's, depended on it.

I wanted and needed to know more about God. I was consumed with difficult questions that begged for answers, and I figured that He just might have them. Admittedly, I went about my quest for very selfish reasons. Somehow, I was convinced that Hunter would go to heaven when he died, and although I knew nothing about heaven or how to get there, I was determined that if Hunter was going, I wanted to go, too.

My mother was diligently searching as well, but unlike me, she sought to know God so Hunter could be healed.

She was convinced that God would heal Hunter. I wasn't.
She prayed for him to be healed. I didn't.

It's not that I never asked God to heal my son. I did. I desperately
wanted Hunter to be healthy like the other boys his age, rough-
housing and throwing the football in the backyard. I just didn't
think it would happen.

My mom wanted healing and I wanted heaven. We were quite
the team.

With no stone left unturned, we charted our course and pursued our goal with different motives but the same passion. We
would have done anything and everything to help Hunter. And
we did, much to our dismay at times.

When Hunter was six months old, we heard about something
called a "healing mass" hosted by a Roman Catholic church near
our home. I was overly protective of Hunter and typically only
took him out of the house for doctor's appointments and family
gatherings at my parents' house. However, Hunter needed to be
healed, and we were desperate, so off to the church we went.
With much anticipation and hope, five of us piled in the van
and headed to church: Hunter; my mother and I; my close friend
Mary; and my best friend from high school, Karyn, who was in
town, and who, as Hunter's godmother, wanted to do whatever
she could to help.

The church was packed but we managed to squeeze into a pew
in the back. As I looked around, I was amazed. *Where did all of
these people come from, and why are they here?* I wondered. A few
familiar hymns were sung and then such a grandiose introduction
was made, you would've thought the pope had come to Western
New York. The majestic ovation the holy man received when he
walked out onto the altar was fit for a king. I don't remember if he

was a priest, a bishop, or a member of some other pontifical rank. I do remember, however, that he was dressed in what looked like a royal robe, he was from Ireland, and from what they said, he had the power to heal.

Because none of us had ever been to a healing mass, we had no idea what to expect. I glanced over at Karyn a few times during the service and the look on her face expressed exactly how I felt. I wanted to leave. But it wasn't about me; Hunter needed to be healed, so we stayed.

After an hour had passed, Hunter started to fuss and cry, so rather than disturb the people around us, we snuck into the quiet room at the back of the church. It was impossible to concentrate on what the holy healer from Ireland was saying, so we just focused on trying to calm Hunter down.

"Mom, let's just go," I pleaded. "Hunter doesn't want to be here, and I don't know what else to do."

"We can't leave now...." my mother began. Then a kind but strange woman interrupted her: "Give the baby to me. I'll calm the child down."

Before I could respond, the woman scooped Hunter out of my arms. My mother and I looked at each other in shock. I glanced over at Karyn and Mary, and they, too, were wide-eyed and dumbfounded.

Agitated, I moved to grab Hunter out of the stranger's arms, but my mother beat me to it. Very graciously and politely she took Hunter from the woman. "Thank you for your help, but I'll take him now," my mother said with authority in her voice.

We were all distraught and completely disillusioned with everything by this point. "Jill, let's get out of here," Karyn insisted.

Suddenly I glanced up and noticed that people were starting to congregate around the altar. Lines had formed down every aisle as men, women, and children waited patiently for the priestly man to lay hands on them and pray over them.

"Now what are we supposed to do?" I asked as my mother gently laid my crying son in my arms.

"We've stayed this long—you've got to take Hunter up there," my mother urged.

Despite everything, I was still hopeful that maybe, just maybe, Hunter had a chance, so I carried him toward the altar. What else could I do? I was his mother.

As we apprehensively made our way to the front of the church, I looked around, hoping to spot someone who could point me in the right direction. I noticed people approaching a particular woman to the far left of the altar. She looked as if she was giving instructions, so I went up to her.

At this point Hunter's crying had intensified, and I was doing everything I could to hold back my own tears. "Can you please tell me where I'm supposed to take my son? He is very sick and needs prayer."

With a look of frustration, the woman brazenly responded, "Go to the back of the line. You'll have to wait."

Without hesitation I turned around and headed to the back of the church—I couldn't get away from that woman quickly enough. Didn't she hear Hunter crying and see the look on his little face? The lump in my throat became unbearable, and I was finding it difficult to breathe.

When I finally made my way over to where my mother and friends were standing, I completely broke down.

"What's wrong? What happened?" my mother asked. I could barely talk through the sobs but managed to repeat what the woman said. Determined and angry like a mother bear, my mom made her way back up to the altar, found an usher, and explained to him what had happened. "My infant grandson has been crying for the last two hours," she declared. "He's very sick and can't wait any longer, so can you please take him now?"

Before I knew it, my mother and I were headed back up to the front of the church with Hunter. We followed the usher through the crowd to the left end of the building where fewer people had gathered. I wanted to run out of there as fast as I could, but Hunter needed to be healed, so we stayed. Eventually the healer from Ireland prayed his way toward us. He was old and scruffy and in a peculiar way reminded me of Santa. He didn't ask any questions or talk to us; he just reached out his wrinkled hands, laid them on Hunter's head, and started praying. I don't remember anything he said, but I do remember this: nothing happened. Hunter continued to cry inconsolably, and so did I.

We headed out the door as fast as we could. No one said a word until Karyn eventually spoke: "Those people are a bunch of freaks. We should've never stayed in there as long as we did. Hunter, you're going to be just fine, little buddy."

We all laughed and cried together.

Upon reaching the van, a woman carrying a five-foot crucifix approached us, nearly frightening us half to death. "They sent me out here to pray for the child. They think he can be healed."

Once again, we were astonished and speechless. The woman leaned her enormous cross up against the van and motioned for me to hand Hunter to her. And I did. As I write this, I still can't believe I let her hold Hunter. But I was desperate.

As she prayed over Hunter, I just stood there. I looked at the golf ball–sized rosary beads around her neck and the five-foot crucifix leaning against my van and thought to myself, *Is she nuts? What in the—are we doing here?* (I used to swear every now and then.) *Why am I letting this strange woman hold my son?* I felt so trapped in the weirdness of everything and just wanted this crazy escapade to be over. We didn't pray along because we didn't know what to do, but as soon as the woman was finished, I snatched Hunter away and got in the van.

After we were safely headed home, far away from all the healers, I burst out crying and protested, "What if that woman was one of God's angels and she really did want to heal Hunter? What if God sent her? I had to let her hold him."

Many tears were shed, and a lot of hope faded that night. No one said much on the way home; I'm sure we were all trying to process everything. The last thing I remember that evening was what my dear friend Mary said as she hugged me good-bye: "At least we tried, Jill, right? And now we know."

Know what? I thought. *Know that people go to crazy extremes out of desperation? Know that however well meaning these people might be, they didn't have a clue about what was best for me and my son? Know that my son is suffering from a disease I've never heard of and there's no cure?* My heart and mind were inundated with questions.

Thankfully, in spite of my confusion, my search for hope and for God continued. I pressed on for Hunter's sake and never gave up. And then, miraculously, in the very midst of Hunter's suffering, the indescribable joy his life brought our family began to overshadow my desire for his healing. Of course I wanted his struggles to end and longed for him to be a healthy, growing boy. However, his life was about so much more than his health. I didn't let God's decision to heal him or not consume me. No, I didn't give up...I gave in. I gave in to a better plan and purpose for Hunter's life. I surrendered my hopes and dreams for Hunter to the God who was weaving a more beautiful tapestry both behind the scenes and before our very eyes for our entire family.

A few months after our healing mass experience, my mother's younger brother, Mark, came over to visit us. He was a born-again Christian. I only knew a few Christians at the time who called themselves "born again," and for some reason, I always felt uncomfortable around them; I just never felt I measured up to their standards. Even though I didn't know what those standards were, I was convinced I was way off, so I tried to avoid them as much as possible.

My understanding of what it meant to be a Christ-follower was jaded and far from accurate. I assumed the pious types were judgmental without realizing I was just as guilty of judging them. Like most unbelievers, I also thought Christians spent all their time walled up in a steeple-topped building singing hymns and beating their Bibles. As horrible as it sounds, I imagined that people serious about God were terribly boring because they had nowhere else to turn for enjoyment in life. There was no way that God could be remotely exciting—at least not according to my definition of excitement at the time.

I was in for a rude awakening.

My uncle Mark was the first person to ever share the details of the gospel story with me—the story of our sinful nature, our need for a Savior, and God's amazing love displayed through the birth, death, and resurrection of Jesus. Mark loved Jesus in a way that I had never witnessed before. He'd been through his share of deep heartbreak and yet was still more passionate for Christ than anyone I knew.

During our many visits together we discussed the tough questions most people ask when tragedy strikes: Why does God allow suffering? Where is God in all of this? Most importantly, why Hunter? Mark didn't always have an answer, and he never tried to appease my doubts with empty platitudes. "I don't know why God is allowing Hunter to go through all this," he'd say, "but I do know that God is real and He loves you. He loves Hunter more than you can imagine."

"How do you know how God loves?" I'd ask.

"Well, first of all, the Bible tells us in the book of John that God loves us so much that He gave His one and only Son for us. If we believe in Jesus and all that He has done for us through His death on the cross, then not only are our sins forgiven, we will eventually spend eternity with Him."

Mark was always mindful not to go too far or get too deep. I hadn't yet accepted Christ as my Savior and didn't fully understand what that meant. And like many non-Christians, I was intimidated and uncomfortable with all the Jesus talk, and he knew this. My body language and facial expressions said it all.

Thankfully, Mark knew when he was in danger of going overboard. Even so, during most of our conversations I found myself craving more. I longed for more of Mark's hope, more of his uncommon joy. Although I struggled with the born-again thing, my desire for heaven and the God behind it all deepened with every conversation.

He and I spent a lot of time talking about a "righteous man" named Job, found in the Old Testament book named after him. The unprecedented amount of pain and heartache Job and his wife had to endure led to some deep conversations about loss and grief. "I can't even imagine what that must have been like for Job," I told Mark. "I love Erin and Hunter so much. The thought of losing them scares me to death. Job lost all ten of his children."

Of all the things that Mark said, there's one thing I will never forget for as long as I live: "Jill, as much as you love your children—and I know you do—you will never know what real love is until you know the love of God through His Son, Jesus."

Initially I was offended and couldn't imagine a love greater than a mother's love for her children—than my love for Erin and Hunter. It was impossible for me to grasp at the time. Still, I was intrigued. How could I come to know this greater love?

Questions like this flooded my mind during Uncle Mark's visits. However, it wasn't so much what Mark said as what I saw and how I felt when I was with him. His life overflowed with joy, and his smile was contagious. In the midst of the sorrow swallowing our family, my uncle was like a breath of fresh air. His love for Jesus was intoxicating, radical, and intimidating all at the same time. I wanted what he had and continued to pursue it with abandon.

Eventually, my search for God took a definitive turn.

When Hunter was a baby, the winter months in Western New York were horrible for him because of RSV and other nasty viruses to which he was easily susceptible. So we would pack up our entire family and head to South Florida for most of the season. We became snowbirds at an early age and enjoyed every minute of it. My uncle Jim and aunt Patsy lived in Fort Myers, Florida, and did all the house-rental legwork for us so that all we had to do was walk through and decide which house to rent.

Like my uncle Mark, Jim and Patsy were also Christians. Upon returning to their home one afternoon after house hunting, I started sobbing. I think the weight of everything was wearing me down and I just had to let go. Erin was with me at the time, and in her sweet, four-year-old innocence she tried her best to console me. "What's wrong, Mommy? Everything's going to be okay, right, Mommy?"

As she put her arms around me and hugged me, tears continued to flow. *I have to be strong. Pull yourself together, Jill. You need to be strong for Erin.* The sound of my aunt and uncle approaching roused me to compose myself. It was obvious that I'd been crying, though, and so they probed in their caring way: "Jill, what's wrong?" Without hesitation I poured out everything I had kept bottled up for so long. The thoughts came tumbling out: "I don't want Hunter to die. Why does he have to suffer so much? Why won't God heal him? I don't understand all this God stuff. If Hunter's going to heaven, I want to go, too. I want to be there." As I continued to ramble on desperately, Erin stood next to me and held my hand. I should have sheltered her from my outcry, but I didn't.

I was desperate. I wanted hope and heaven so badly I would've carried around a five-foot crucifix if I had to. I was tired of running; the anguish of searching had wiped me out. I was down for the count, and my aunt and uncle knew it, so when I finally stopped to breathe, Jim and Patsy motioned for me to come into the living room. "Let's just pray right now. Jill, God knows what you need," they said. "You need Him. You need Jesus."

I dropped to my knees, and as we knelt down to pray, I looked at Erin. She was crying. The look on her face broke my heart.

Knowing that I wouldn't have the slightest idea what to pray, Uncle Jim told me to repeat after him, and so I did. While I don't remember my exact words, I knew what I felt was real, and I'll never forget it.

Now, as I vividly recall those moments on my knees crying out to God, I realize with even greater conviction what I couldn't possibly have understood then. It wasn't about how or what I prayed—as if spewing "magical," spiritual-sounding words could make any difference at all. It wasn't about my desperation or need for hope. It wasn't even about acknowledging my sin and repenting, because I didn't understand the breadth of my sin at the time or what godly repentance was. Nothing I did or didn't do could possibly alter the course of my life and eternity. I could barely function enough to make sense of the most meaningless of tasks. I was a complete wreck.

It was just Jesus—what He did and the power of God's love working through Him to save me…to save our entire family.

Just Jesus.

I didn't find the hope I needed in a husband who was as desperate for that hope as I was.

I didn't find God at a healing mass.

I didn't discover Him in church tradition I never understood to begin with, or while growing up in parochial school.

I didn't find Him in my desperate search for hope and meaning in the midst of all my pain.

As strange as it may seem, I caught a glimpse of Him in the midst of my son's suffering.

I felt Him in the warmth of my tears.

And oddly enough, I heard His call in the stillness of complete silence. I felt His touch when I dropped to my knees.

In Jim's Own Words

When Jill became a Christian it really didn't sink in right away. I never hung out with the Christians on the team, so I didn't know what to expect from her. I remember telling Jill, "You can do whatever you want, but don't push that stuff on me."

It didn't bother me that Jill had turned to God; I just didn't want her to expect me to change, too. I heard enough about Jesus in the locker room, I didn't want to hear it from my wife, too. And I sure didn't want Him pushed on me.

I always felt very uncomfortable around the Christians on the team. Though the guys probably didn't think they were being overly pushy, they were, and I didn't like it. They weren't all that interested in me; they just wanted me to become a Christian.

Except for Frank Reich.

I knew Frank before he gave his life to Jesus. He was my roommate for road games and we spent a lot of time together. "Frankie J" never pushed his faith on me. It's a good thing, too, because I don't think we could've worked together if he had.

Whenever I heard the guys talking about God in the locker room I tried to avoid the conversation. I had more important things on my mind, like winning football games and going to the Big Tree (a small bar near Ralph Wilson Stadium) with my buddies after practice. I didn't have time for all that God stuff. And besides, because of Hunter's disease, I was mad at God. There was no way I was going to be able to hear people when they said, "You're a chosen father, Jim. Maybe God picked you to be Hunter's dad because He knew you would do something about it."

I got so sick and tired of hearing that I was a "chosen father." Even though I knew people were just trying to encourage me, it didn't make me feel any better. I didn't want to accept that the son I'd always wanted, born on my birthday, was sick. Knowing that Hunter would never be able to catch a pass from Daddy or suit up in a bantam football jersey crushed me. I had dreamt about all the things I would do with my son. I planned on us going hunting and fishing as fathers and sons do. I wanted to coach his sports teams and teach him the right way to grip a football. Hunter would never be all I had hoped he would be.

It took a long time for me to realize that good would come from our tragedy. Eventually I did. But even knowing and seeing all the good that came from Hunter's life doesn't take away the pain of wishing things could've been different.

Initially I tried to run from it all as much as I could. I had retired from the game I love two weeks before Hunter was born. It was perfect timing, really, because I had plans for our family. Shortly after my retirement, NBC Sports wanted to hire me. At first I wasn't interested, but after Hunter got sick I needed to do something. My job with NBC Sports had me traveling all over the place doing color analysis for games. After two seasons I left NBC and started working for ESPN. I traveled to Bristol, Connecticut, for the show every week and was often distracted with my responsibilities there. Being away from home took my mind off of everything temporarily but . . . I still thought about Hunter often and wished I could help him.

Many times on the road, by myself in my hotel room, I would cry and ask WHY? I wasn't comfortable showing my emotions, but sometimes I had to let them out . . . but only when I was by myself. Jill never realized I cared as much as I did because I never showed my emotions in front of her and the kids. That was how I was brought up. You never cry. No way. I was born and raised in a family of six boys. I never wanted to cry in front of my dad or my five brothers, so I didn't.

I was hoping for a cure for Hunter. After we went public with his diagnosis, I was hopeful that maybe there was a treatment out there somewhere. But there wasn't, and Hunter continued to suffer.

I hated watching my son struggle. It killed me. I tried not to think about it.

Chapter 6

Change

Following Hunter's diagnosis, my life and the life of every member of our family changed drastically. We soon discovered that change is extremely hard; it rips us out of our comfort zones. Change takes us to unknown places where fear is palpable and the longing for normalcy and the safety of the familiar is consuming.

Krabbe disease is ruthless. The prognosis is grim and the average life expectancy for a child with Krabbe is fourteen months. Its victims typically suffer from severe and rapid deterioration of mental and motor functions, become deaf and blind, and eventually succumb to the disease as a result of pneumonia or heart failure. As Krabbe progresses and the sufferers deteriorate, the need for specialized medical intervention—as well as various therapies, medications, and medical apparatuses—increases.

By the time Hunter was a mere four months old, it was already evident that he was unable to achieve the physical and social developmental milestones that infants his age normally do. Hunter's inability to move on his own kept him from lifting his head, kicking his legs, and reaching with his arms as healthy infants do. Hunter couldn't swallow either, necessitating his need for a suction machine and feeding pump. Suction machine...what in the world is that? I remember how afraid I was when we were first introduced to the apparatus and taught how to use it. It was horrible. The machine was so loud, and the thought of sucking sputum out of the back of my son's throat was very unsettling.

Although the suction machine, feeding pump, oxygen tanks, wheelchair, stander, and other equipment we needed helped Hunter live, the adjustments were difficult for all of us, no one more than Hunter. Eventually we embraced these changes, but it took time.

As Hunter's disease progressed and he required intense specialized medical intervention in every area of his life, his extreme needs demanded that we open up our home and lives to complete strangers. By this time I was used to life in a fishbowl; it came with the territory. Throughout most of Jim's NFL career, and especially during the four Super Bowl years, we could not escape the glare of the spotlight. But this was different—it was our home. It was our son, our family, and we didn't know how to handle life and cope with a desperately sick child. We wanted to run away from people, not invite them into our lives and pain. But we were also determined to do anything and everything to help Hunter. If that meant allowing strangers into our home on a daily basis, reluctantly revealing the deeply personal details of the worst time in our lives, then we would.

When Hunter was an infant, I was initially reluctant to let anyone other than my mother hold him. Even Jim got reprimanded a number of times for not holding him the right way. I was radically overprotective—to a fault. But my son's deteriorating health required the specialized care of professionals. I had the hardest time letting other people take care of Hunter, but he needed what I was unable to give. I wanted to do everything for him, but I didn't know how. Over time I learned to let go—but it wasn't easy.

It took an incredible amount of patience for us to adjust to the coming and going of Hunter's caregivers. He had a tight schedule from the moment he got up until bedtime. Hunter wasn't your typical sick kid; he had a rare genetic disease most people had never heard of. Our therapists, nurses, and caregivers—our team affectionately known as Team Hunter—were learning, too. We responded to his needs as they arose, and everything depended on how he was feeling. Our home revolved around Hunter, so we learned to hold our agendas loosely. We were all being schooled as we went, and I learned everything I possibly could to better care for him.

Already on the scene when Hunter was born was Reggie. "Reggamatic," as we called her because of her Energizer Bunny–meets-old-school work ethic, was one of our nannies. But she was much more than that. Reggie loved Hunter and the girls. She had come to work for us when Erin was a toddler. Jim said that Reggie was like Aunt Bee from *The Andy Griffith Show*. Her blonde hair was always whipped up into a molded beehive and her make-up was perfect. Whenever she took a break, which wasn't very often, she would freshen up her lipstick. "You never know when you might get discovered," she would proclaim with a laugh.

Reggie spent a lot of time with Hunter. She loved reading to him and massaging his body. Hunter loved listening to Reggie talk and sing, and he always fell asleep when she gave him a back rub. When Hunter was three years old he learned how to communicate with his eyes, a huge breakthrough in helping us care for him. Reggie gets most of the credit for this—she taught Hunter how to blink once for yes, something she takes great pride in to this day.

Amy, Hunter's physical therapist, and Kathy, his occupational therapist, were the first to "invade" our home after Hunter became ill. As harsh as it sounds, that's exactly how we felt initially. Living with Hunter's disease was hard enough and exposing our pain and inadequacies to complete strangers made us very uncomfortable. I didn't want to reveal the enormity of our struggles and fears to anyone other than family; it was just too hard being so vulnerable. With the way Hunter and his daily needs consumed me, I was convinced I didn't have time to forge new relationships or invest in anyone else's life. Yet somehow, as new members of our growing team shared part of their lives with Hunter, the capacity of my heart grew to accommodate new friendships. Friendships rooted in a love and camaraderie beyond my wildest expectations.

Team Hunter was family. We all grew to love and care about each other to a depth that surprised every one of us. We depended on each other to maximize Hunter's care and learned to work together in a way that allowed the Kelly household to look and feel like home again. It was truly amazing, especially because our team consisted of all women—except Hunter and Jim, of course. How we were able to keep the emotional estrogen roller coaster in check (for the most part) is a mystery for sure.

Don't get me wrong; we all had our moments, or days, and they weren't pretty. But the respect and love we had for each other in our determination to provide Hunter with the utmost care possible kept us from allowing this world's burdens and the issues of our individual lives to hinder our team efforts. Hunter needed us to focus, to work together, to love and live and spread joy. Somehow—we did.

In Jim's Own Words

After we found out that Hunter would need nurses and therapists around the clock, I realized that our household had to adapt. And that adjustment was hard—very hard. I had always tried to maintain some sort of privacy throughout my NFL career. But it was almost impossible. Cars would inch by my house hoping to get a picture. Some people would even come up and peek through the front windows and then drive away. It really got ridiculous at times.

When Jill and I started a family, I became even more protective of our privacy. But that all changed when Hunter got sick. Someone was always at the house. Very seldom did we have dinner with just us because there was always at least one other person—and sometimes two—around. I used to joke with Hunter and say, "We're surrounded by a bunch of hens again, HB." And we were. It was just me and Hunter and a bunch of women. We were completely outnumbered, which was difficult for a lot of reasons.

At first it really bothered me that Jill and I could seldom be alone by ourselves or with our kids, but I got used to it. In fact, there were so many people coming in and out of the house that I eventually told everyone not to ring the doorbell anymore.

It didn't take long for me to realize how important Team Hunter was to our entire family. We really were a team, and even though I wasn't leading the way, I knew my son was getting the best care possible. Of course I wished the circumstances were different, but Team Hunter touched all of our lives in many special ways.

———

While not a therapist, nurse, or professional caregiver, there was one very special person who became a vital part of Hunter's life and whose contribution to the change we all experienced was like an unexpected treasure. His name was Robert. Robert was the son of Elizabeth, Hunter's physical therapist after Amy left to have a baby. When Hunter was three, Elizabeth brought Robert over to play, and a most extraordinary friendship was born.

Robert had no problem getting right down on the floor with Hunter and playing as if his heart would burst. Laughter would ring through the house when the boys were together, and there was no end to what they would dream up to do. The boys were... boys, in the greatest sense of the word. Through Robert, Hunter could do all the things he wanted to do; through Hunter, Robert could imagine the most wonderful adventures. They were connected in a profound way, in the way that really matters. They were connected by love.

Here are Robert's thoughts, in his own words, about his friendship with Hunter.

My mom is a physical therapist and started seeing Hunter when we were both babies. Before we even met, we started sharing our toys, using my mom as a shuttle service. I'd send some dinosaurs with her to use during therapy with Hunter, and he would send some Rescue Heroes back. When I was three, Mrs. Kelly invited me to come over during therapy to play with the toys in person. I was sort of nervous because I didn't often meet kids, but I was also excited because I wanted to make a new friend. When I walked into the house, I hid behind my mother. Then we went into the playroom where Hunter was. I peeked out and saw Hunter. As soon as I saw him, I thought he was a good guy and hoped we would be great friends.

I realize now that our friendship was really special, but at the time Hunter was just a regular kid to me. Being friends with Hunter wasn't different than being friends with any other kid on the block. He couldn't talk, but he certainly didn't have any trouble letting me know what he wanted to play. He'd blink his eyes or keep them wide open. He even waved to me a few times.

We did all of the things kids do—we played, talked, watched movies, read books together, and had lots of fun. We built forts in his family room and shone flashlights on the ceiling. We played card games. I couldn't read Hunter's mind or anything, but he seemed to really have fun when we were together.

My favorite day ever with Hunter was when we were outside on the deck playing with Silly String. We were playing Spider-Man and had these super-cool web-shooters. We both sprayed each other, then we sprayed Hunter's nurse, then my mom, and then we had fun spraying Hunter's little sister, Camryn. I didn't have a little sister, so Hunter shared his with me. We had a great time! There was Silly String everywhere, but mostly on Camryn.

There were lots of ways Hunter and I were the same:

- We were the same age (almost).
- We were the same size. (We measured—but my feet were bigger.)
- We both liked horses, Spider-Man, and football.
- We were both smart and liked to read good books.
- We were always happy to see each other.

There were also some ways that Hunter and I were different:

- He had Krabbe Leukodystrophy; I have food allergies.
- He had a dad who was a famous football player; my dad is just a regular guy.
- He was older than me by six months. (See above.)

- *He liked to wear his hair spiky; I kept mine flat.*
- *My head was bigger (physically, not mentally).*
- *I wore glasses; Hunter didn't.*

Sometimes, I would try out some of Hunter's special equipment to make sure it was okay for him. I did that because I loved him and didn't want him to get hurt. It was cool going into his equipment. I especially liked trying out the Trixie Lift, which was a kind of roller-coaster ride with Hunter at the controls. Funny—he had no interest in riding the lift himself—he merely wanted to take me for a spin. I tried out his new wheelchair, too, and let his mom take me for a ride in the new van so she wouldn't be as worried about Hunter when it was his turn.

That's what friends do, and Hunter was my best friend.

What an amazing young man.

Robert's words make me cry and yet fill me with great joy. They remind me that while change is difficult, it can also be the uncharted pathway to uncommon joy and unexpected miracles.

Hunter taught us how to live with change and anticipate it. Change we grudgingly succumbed to kicking and screaming… and change we somehow welcomed with open arms. He taught us that the unknown doesn't always have to be scary. Though initially fearful, we learned to expect and embrace the uncomfortable and the unfamiliar. We learned to surrender the need to control because so many things were out of our control. And even though we didn't know what the unknown held, we learned to trust the One who holds the unknown.

Chapter 7

Hunter and His Sisters

A few months after Hunter was diagnosed with Krabbe disease, we had Erin Marie tested. Dr. Duffner wanted to determine whether or not Erin was a carrier of the deficient gene.

At first I was reluctant and anxious. Even though Dr. Duffner assured me that it was highly unlikely that Erin could have the disease, I was scared to death. When we took Erin to Children's Hospital to have her blood work done, she was such a big girl. Almost three at the time, she didn't fully understand what was going on or why they had to stick her with a needle to draw blood. But she walked in with confidence and didn't flinch or cry throughout the entire process. I was amazed at her demeanor and proud of her for being so courageous.

A flood of dreadful outcomes crossed my mind as we waited to hear the results. I imagined Dr. Duffner calling us into her office again to tell us that Erin, too, had Krabbe Leukodystrophy. Waiting was horrible. The longer we had to wait, the more anxious I became. Finally, after what seemed like an eternity, the phone rang. Reggie answered it and called me from the kitchen: "Jill, Dr. Duffner's on the phone." Erin and Hunter were cuddled next to each other on the living room couch watching *Franklin the Turtle*. Erin's treasured "fruit blankie" was spread out evenly between them and her "juice ba ba" was tucked between the couch cushions. (Whenever they snuggled she made sure everything was perfect.)

My heart started to race as I hopped up from the couch and went into the kitchen. Reggie handed me the phone and kept the kids occupied so I could talk in private. Dr. Duffner was not much for small talk and got right to the point: "Jill, Erin is not a carrier. Her enzyme levels are completely normal, so she'll never have to worry. This is great news, isn't it?" Then she softened and added, "So, how's my Little Rabbit doing today?"

Dr. Duffner had nicknamed Hunter "Little Rabbit" months before. She was very affectionate toward him, and her bedside manner was always gracious and loving.

After I hung up the phone, I ran into the bathroom to compose myself so Erin wouldn't see me and ask, as she often did, "Why are you crying, Mommy?" My tears came freely, and they were mixed with emotion. I was thankful to hear the good news, and yet, at the same time, my heart ached for Hunter. Why did he have to suffer?

———

Although Jim and I spent very little intimate time together because of the bitterness eroding my heart, still, we both desired to have more children. We were terrified, too, of the possibility that we might conceive another child with Krabbe disease. Yet our desire for a baby outweighed our fear and we tried anyway. And somehow we managed to be alone enough to get pregnant with our third child.

On October 21, 1998, I took two pregnancy tests (just to be sure!) and wrote the following in my journal that day:

I'm pregnant! I can hardly believe it. I'm excited and yet sort of scared. Erin and Hunter need a brother or sister. This is going to be wonderful—I just know it. I'll have to start taking better care of myself. So many thoughts are flooding my mind right now. If it's a boy—I like Noah James Kelly. I love how that sounds. When I asked Erin Marie what she would name the baby if it were a girl, she said "Casey." I don't think so.

Wait till Jim finds out. He really wants us to be pregnant again. He'll be so excited. I told my mom, and of course we both cried. God has blessed us with another baby. I hope the baby will be okay. Whatever happens, happens—He will be with me every step of the way.

I just looked over at a pillow in Hunter's room that has "Trust in the Lord with all your heart" embroidered on it. I will! This is going to be great! I just know it is!

When I was about four months pregnant, Dr. Duffner suggested we have the baby tested through amniocentesis. Because we'd already had a child with Krabbe, we were able to find out before the birth of any subsequent children whether or not they have the disease. With every child Jim and I have there is a 25 percent chance that he or she will be born with Krabbe disease and a 50 percent chance that the baby will be a carrier.

Unfortunately, we lived in the spotlight. So when it became public knowledge that I was pregnant with our third child, incredibly, we received some nasty letters. We were stunned by the cruelty of some of the comments. People found it necessary to tell us that they thought our having another child was a disgrace and that we should be ashamed of ourselves for taking the risk.

What were we supposed to do? Get an abortion? Stop having children? We felt it was incredibly arrogant and sad that people who have never walked in our shoes found it so easy to pass judgment. And as much as we might have wanted to respond to the irresponsible comments, it wouldn't have made any difference. People are people. Besides, how could they have possibly understood the inconceivable joy Hunter's life brought to our family? How could those who only read or saw the portion of our lives framed by the media actually know the bigger, almost indescribable, reality?

As crazy as it may sound, I didn't stress out over the outcome of the baby's test results. I had an unexplainable peace throughout my entire pregnancy.

Our family was in South Florida when we got the word. I'll never forget that day. Just thinking about it makes me cry.

It was a gorgeous, sunny afternoon with a gentle breeze drifting in off the Gulf of Mexico. While Jim and my dad prepared the grill for dinner, the rest of us were hanging out at the beach. Hunter loved the ocean. And even though we had to keep him out of the sun as much as possible, he still enjoyed the sand and the waves.

Erin was busy building a sandcastle and Hunter was relaxing on a lounge chair under the cabana with Grammie when my grandfather shouted down to us from the wooden walkway, "Jill, your doctor's on the phone." I jumped up from my chair and ran to meet him. Waving the portable phone as he handed it to me, he said, "Jill, it's Hunter's doctor, Dr. Duffner. It's something about the baby."

As soon as he said "baby," I felt faint. A profound peace about everything had enveloped me until the moment Grandpa Jack handed me the phone. With one hand on my belly and the other holding the phone, I stood there as a rush of anguish swept through my entire body and fear slammed into my heart. *What if the baby has Krabbe disease?* I put the phone up to my ear and heard myself weakly stammer, "Hello."

Without hesitation Dr. Duffner declared the good news: "The baby is fine, Jill. She is a carrier, but her enzyme levels are near normal." Before she could say another word, I interrupted and asked, "Are you sure? Are you sure she's going to be okay?" As Dr. Duffner continued to reassure me, I started sobbing. After I hung up the phone I walked back toward the cabana where Hunter and my mother were sitting.

I was overjoyed and thankful about the news, but despair and sorrow unfortunately crept in and covered my heart. *Why Hunter? Why our only son?*

I didn't want the kids to see me crying, so I quickly pulled myself together before rejoining the family. Confused and overcome by the intense pain and joy of the moment, I was silent when I first sat back down. My mother knew I didn't want to say anything in front of Hunter. I didn't want him to feel bad, so I knelt beside him, wrapped him in my arms, and just held him. It was bittersweet. I was so thankful the baby (who turned out to be Camryn) was going to be okay, that she was just a carrier. But at the same time, my heart was crushed all over again for Hunter.

———

One of my greatest challenges was making time for all three kids. I made every effort to spend as much time as possible with my daughters, but Hunter's needs often required immediate attention, so inevitably I spent more time with him. I struggled with guilt and fervently prayed that God would help me to balance my time and energy. Even though I did the best I could, it was very hard and emotionally draining.

At least once a month I tried to set aside a special day for each child. We named our special days "Mommy & Erin Day," "Mommy & Hunter Day," and "Mommy & Camryn Day." When it was Mommy & Erin Day, Erin got to choose what we did from start to finish. If she wanted to go to the movies, we went to the movies. If she wanted to go to the playground, we went to the playground. It was her time with Mommy to do whatever her heart desired.

Depending on what was easiest for Hunter, my mother would either take the other two kids to her house, or she would watch them at ours. We did whatever we had to so that each child's special day was loaded with fun. I looked forward to those days so much. Yet in spite of our efforts to bring some sort of normalcy into our children's lives, their lives were far from normal.

We tried to include the girls in Hunter's daily activities and therapies so they understood how to work all his machines and pumps. As a result, many times Erin and Camryn would pretend their baby dolls had Krabbe disease. As apprehensive as I was about letting them use Hunter's supplies for play, I couldn't help but encourage them. There was something beautiful, though painful, in watching my daughters mimic what I struggled to do every day.

Their babies were tube-fed and suctioned, just like Hunter, so they needed feeding bags, syringes, and suction machines. I'd tape the end of the feeding bags to their babies' bellies so they could pretend like they were really giving them food. Rather than using formula, as we did with Hunter, the girls filled their dolls' bags with water.

They had watched us enough to know exactly what to do with everything, including the oxygen. Although positioning the nasal cannula inside the dolls' little plastic noses and around their ears was a challenge, we managed. I also let the girls attach oxygen tubing to empty tanks. And while the tanks weren't that heavy, watching little Camryn strap one over her shoulder and lug it around was humorous and heartwarming.

The girls had hours of fun with their Krabbe babies. I didn't want to interrupt their playtime, so I'd watch them from a distance and listen.

"What's your baby's name?" Erin would ask her sister.

"Her name is Courtney," Camryn would respond joyfully, "and she's very sick because she has Krabbe disease."

"Oh, my daughter has Krabbe, too," Erin would reply. "When was Courtney diagnosed?"

"Well, we found out that she was sick a couple of weeks ago. What about you?"

"My baby had Krabbe when she was born," Erin would say, cradling her doll. "Does your baby get chest therapy?"

As kids often do, they carried on for hours. While I watched them play, I wondered what Hunter was thinking as he listened to his sisters. I often pondered over how extraordinary it was that my daughters chose to pretend that their dolls were sick rather than healthy. Was that their way of expressing their love for their sick brother? Or in some strange way were they revealing their pain in the only way they knew how?

Little did they know or understand how difficult it was to take care of Hunter. And yet maybe the incredible joy we all felt blinded their eyes to the crushing pain.

Camryn was very affectionate toward her older brother. It didn't even cross her mind that she might be a little too rough with him. From the time she could toddle around on her own, she always made her way over to wherever Hunter was. Whatever he was doing, Camryn wanted to do, too. Like a little shadow, she constantly wanted to be next to her big brother. If Hunterboy was lying down, stretching and exercising, she was, too. If he was upright in his stander, she wanted to be strapped in when he got out. If Hunter had school, Camryn wanted to learn, too. Hunter's therapists, teachers, and nurses were patient and mindful of Cam's desires and tried to include her as much as possible.

A few times, to our amusement and dismay, Camryn tried to get a little too involved in Hunter's care. Once we caught her on camera trying to give her brother chest therapy. With percussor in hand, she laid her head next to Hunter on the couch and put her hand on his back. If we hadn't intervened, I'm sure she would've started pounding away. Oddly enough, I think Hunter would've liked it, at least for a few minutes.

He loved his sisters. Whenever the girls were around, Hunter would raise his eyebrows and his eyes would light up and sparkle. His body also seemed to relax whenever his sisters would snuggle up next to him. An indescribable, unspoken love radiated from my children whenever they were together. Watching them was truly incredible.

As day after day, month after month, and then year after year went by, I could see that the girls were developing emotionally and spiritually in a way few children get to experience. A significant part of who the girls were, and who they are today, is because of their incredible relationship with their brother, Hunter. God was allowing them to *vicariously* experience the physical pain of suffering while at the same time allowing them to *actually* feel the intensity of unconditional love. They daily witnessed what disease can do to the frail human body, and as a result they appreciated the blessing of every breath.

They were learning how to be compassionate, caring, and merciful in the school of heartbreak. Even at a young age, they already knew more about life and death than most of us learn in a lifetime.

Chapter 8

Hunter at One and Two

I journaled as much as possible throughout Hunter's life, writing mostly about special things only a mommy would appreciate or milestones only I would consider huge. Things like a good or bad night's sleep, losing teeth, good bowel movements, holding hands. I also chronicled the continued brokenness of a mother's heart as my love for Hunter grew ever deeper. I prayed a lot in my journals as well. So in the midst of most of my entries describing a typical or not-so-typical day for my son, I would break out in prayer and praise. Praise for all that was and all I hoped would be.

My journals are full of intimate memories. Its pages are stained with tears of joy and sorrow—and my morning coffee. They are torn and wrinkled with fear and failure, hope and heaven. Exclamation marks, circles, hearts, underlines, and scribbles are all part of this well-worn evidence of a mother's plight to save her son and, ultimately, let him go.

Answered and unanswered prayers are recorded in my journals, too, as well as the laughter, the sobbing, the screams of anguish, and the silence. The silence speaks the loudest. Sharing my journals is like giving away remnants of my heart, a quilted patchwork of vibrant hopes and dreams held together by a love as singular as the silence that could not inhibit it. Yet words fall short and always will. The inexpressible love, hope, joy, and sorrow I have as a result of being Hunter's mommy permeate every strand of who I am.

Because journaling is so personal, journals can often give the reader a perspective on the events being chronicled that other forms of writing cannot. So in this chapter, and the four that follow, I've chosen to give you a glimpse of Hunter through a chronological gathering of my journal entries. Hopefully these will enable you to see his life through a new lens and appreciate how truly extraordinary his life was. I've never been this transparent or risked sharing my heart and my Hunter like this, until now.

Those of us who knew Hunter will tell you that he changed us in profound ways. The grass somehow appeared greener, and the array of beauty that colors our world and the intricate details of creation became more vibrant. Simple things we were usually too busy to appreciate filled us with gratitude because, incredibly, God used the simplicity of the common to show us how uncommon simple things really are. Hunter loved life...all of it. His suffering didn't take away from his ability to enjoy life; it only made him enjoy what he could that much more.

Year One, 1997–1998

> *July 14, 1997—Hunter turned five months old today and weighs 14 pounds, 6 ounces. We celebrate every day with him because we don't know how long he'll be with us. Every day we try to encourage him to smile by tickling his cute, puffy toes and smooching his neck. We act goofy and make silly faces for him, but he's still very irritable. Poor little guy. I guess it's*

just too hard for him to smile. I think he's beautiful, though,
even when he cries.

What's making my boy so miserable? Dr. Duffner doesn't
know what part of Krabbe causes irritability. I just hope
he's not in pain. If Hunter's crying because he's in pain...
I can't even go there. Lately he's been twitching a lot too.
I wonder why.

We spend a lot of time trying to keep Hunter busy with
toys, music, and massages throughout the day. He calms
down some whenever we kiss his feet and rub his legs. We still
try to give him a bottle even though he has a feeding tube
now. I'm hoping he'll be able to taste and swallow at least for
a little longer. Hunter loves his moon-and-stars pacifier and
knows when we try to give him a different one—little stinker.
He won't move his mouth at all if it's any other pacifier. I'm
so thankful he hasn't lost his ability to suck yet.

At least one doctor calls us every day to make sure
everything is going okay. We never know when we'll have to
take Hunter to the hospital because the effects of this
disease sneak up on you. As time goes by, more of Hunter's
normal bodily functions will shut down, necessitating his
need for continuous medical intervention. In the meantime,
even though I dread going there, I'm so thankful that we
can take Hunter to Children's Hospital. I wish we knew more
about this horrible disease.

August 14, 1997—Hunter's six-month birthday is today. He
weighs 14 pounds, 13 ounces. He's less irritable now, though
he hasn't smiled yet. Maybe the medication they put him
on to help with his irritability and seizures is what keeps
him so out of it now. We need to find out. And ever since his
operation to have his feeding tube in, he hasn't opened his

eyes. People keep asking me if he's asleep. I know he's awake, but how do I explain to them what I don't understand? Why are Hunter's eyes closed? I don't know. I have no idea what's going on inside his precious, diseased body. I'd do anything to make Krabbe disappear. Hunter's green eyes are so incredible. I wish he would open them. What if he can't? What if he never opens his eyes again?

We had an appointment with Dr. Duffner today at Children's Hospital to discuss the option of a cord blood transplant for Hunter. She said there's talk in the medical community that a transplant might actually stop the progression of Krabbe disease. It's experimental at this point, but she's going to investigate everything and let us know what she finds out. It's the only option out there, so we must consider it. We'll see. We also discussed going "public" with Hunter's situation to see if there might be more help out there for him. This is so horrible. I wish I could take his place....

September 3, 1997—I'm sitting on an airplane returning from Duke University after meeting with Dr. Joanne Kurtzberg regarding a bone marrow/cord blood transplant for Hunter. This has been a very difficult day. I saw so many sick children at Duke, and yet their parents were so pleasant and optimistic. They have so much to deal with, yet they walk around with smiles. It baffled me to see that. I wonder how they do it? I wonder if I will be able to smile soon.

Dr. Kurtzberg doesn't think Hunter's body can withstand the chemotherapy and everything involved in having a cord blood transplant because of all the damage Krabbe has already done to his little body. Even if a transplant could stop the relentless destruction of Krabbe, she estimates that it could take up to a year. Meanwhile, the disease would continue to fully progress with irreversible results, Hunter would still need a feeding tube. He still wouldn't be able to swallow or smile or move his body like a healthy baby. He wouldn't develop or achieve the milestones he's supposed to as a six-month-old. Even the simplest things like reaching for toys, Hunter would never be able to do because he can't hold his little head up or grasp things with his hands. He'll never utter his first word. What if he wants to say "Mama" or "Dada"? He can't. A transplant won't reverse any of that. And it won't save Hunter. So, he won't be getting one.

I'm sad and fearful for Hunter. I just want to hug and kiss him forever. I'm scared to watch him die and I don't know if I can handle it.

September 28, 1997—Well, we're in NYC right now. I'm sitting here in our hotel room, a nervous wreck because tomorrow Jim and I will appear on *The Today Show* to talk about Hunter and Hunter's Hope, the foundation we formed to help children like Hunter. This is way beyond my comfort zone... but we have to do whatever it takes for Hunter. There's no limit—we'll always do whatever it takes to help our son. He needs us. I need him....

January 28, 1998 (Children's Hospital, Buffalo, NY)—We're in the intensive care unit because Hunter has pneumonia. He's hooked up to a ventilator and all sorts of machines and IV medications. I can't even hold him because he's attached to all these tubes.

We've been in here for ten days already. Jim, my mother, and I take turns staying here day and night, and when we're not here, we have to be at home with Erin Marie. One of us is always by Hunter's side—always.

Some people from the hospital asked if we wanted to sign DNR papers in case something happens to Hunter. I don't care what any doctor says or what Krabbe disease will try to do to my son—he needs me and I'm going to fight for him as long as he's living and breathing.

February 14, 1998—It might seem like a typical day but it's not—Hunter's one today. Every day he's here is a celebration of life. He's such a beautiful boy. I could stare at his face all day long.

Erin loves snuggling with her brother. She has no idea that her brother might not live very long. I'm afraid for her... I'm afraid for all of us. This is all so scary and there's so much we don't know and understand.

People are rallying to support Hunter's Hope and our family. It's comforting that people we don't even know, complete strangers, care about helping Hunter and children like him. We need all the support we can get.

Hunter never smiled, and yet he did. For some reason, during the first year of his life we wanted so badly for him to smile. I guess because ordinarily a smile is considered an outward expression of happiness and joy. We had to learn that inward joy could be expressed in other, more profound ways. Just the fact that Hunter was breathing, that he was alive and fighting in his own way to be a part of life, was amazing.

We all learned a lot that first year. I became acutely aware of the fragility and sanctity of life; that life matters, no matter the breadth or quality of it. Life itself is a gift. Every single breath is a treasure.

Hunter treasured life. And his desire to live changed us.

Year Two, 1998–1999

March 2, 1998—Hunter sat in his Kid Kart wheelchair for the first time today. Kathy and Elizabeth positioned him perfectly and he looked like such a big boy in his new ride. Of course, we made a big deal out of it—we make a big deal out of everything. Erin couldn't wait to push him up and down the hallway. I'm sure she'll be asking to push him around every time he's up.

Hunter's equipment usually intimidates me at first, but realizing how much he benefits from it has made me more open and accepting of everything he might need. It's a challenge, but I'm learning.

May 7, 1998—Start feeding, stop feeding, physical therapy, Albuterol, chest therapy, exercise, medication; start feeding, stop feeding, occupational therapy, Tylenol, massage, and Jacuzzi—it's always something. Hunter's routine dictates everything all the time. I just want him to be free. Free from pain and medicine. Free from everything.

I wish I could make everything better, but I can't. I feel so helpless and sometimes hopeless. I'm afraid to leave Hunter, so it's hard for me to go anywhere. When I leave the house, even if only for an hour, I worry about him the entire time I'm gone. This is horrible.

June 17, 1998—It seemed like a miracle happened today with Hunter. He was sitting on Grammie's lap and his legs were dangling freely, and he started to lift his legs up and down all by himself. It was amazing. He pulled his right leg up first, and then his left leg in a circular motion like riding a bicycle. Hunter always tries so hard and he's such a fighter.

August 1, 1998—Hunter's Hope 5K Race was today. We're trying to organize as many events as possible to continue to get the word out about Krabbe disease and other leukodystrophies.

I don't know where we'd be if Jim hadn't played for the Buffalo Bills. We need his fans to rally behind our efforts. What a miracle it would be if we found a cure for Krabbe before that dreadful disease steals Hunter's precious life. Watching him struggle every day will surely put me in the grave. Without him that's where I'd want to be anyway.

We've been trying all sorts of alternative supplements and treatments for Hunter. The list is long: Noni juice, Mannatech, herbs and essential oils, magnetic mats—all sorts of stuff I've never heard of before. Hey, if it works, I'm all for it. But what if none of these things help Hunter? What will we do?

We're desperate. My mom is always searching for ways to help him. I don't know what I'd do without her.

September 27, 1998—Hunter was really sick this morning and slept almost the entire day except for when he was in the Jacuzzi. He was showing off in the water. It's so exciting to watch him try to do little things like moving his head ever so slightly to look up at me. .

Every move Hunter makes is so amazing to me that I

just want to bawl every time. Moments like these tell me he
wants to live; he wants to move. I can see the desperation
in his eyes, and it kills me. We can't help but colobrate every
one of his achievements; everything he does. We rejoice in
the fact that he's alive. He senses our excitement and we
know that it motivates him to forge ahead and keep trying.
It's amazing what a little encouragement can do.

We think Hunter's having a hard time digesting food and
we're very concerned. Hunter's physical therapist always has
great ideas to help him. The other day she molded special
shoes that form to Hunter's feet for him to use while in the
stander. They're so cute. Her name is Elizabeth, and she's
great. To think that I was so apprehensive about her taking
care of Hunter....You never know what change will do.

Erin Marie likes preschool but she misses her brother
when she's gone. They're so cute together. It's really late...
gotta go.

October 5, 1998—I wish I could make this all go away—
Hunter shouldn't have to go through all this. He's on oxygen
pretty much all the time now. This is so hard. What a brave
little pumpkin he is. He struggles from morning to night just
to live. Even though I can't even stand the thought of being
without him, I want him to be in heaven where he'll be happy
and suffer no more. Every time he gets sick, I wonder if he'll
get better or if he'll continue to deteriorate.

I love the way Hunter smells. When I kissed him good-
night tonight, he smelled so fresh and clean. Grammie put
Erin's shirt on Hunter for bed...we were all laughing...I think
Hunter was laughing too. Imagine that—laughing without
making a sound. I don't understand it all, but I know it's true.
I love him. I love him. I love him.

November 24, 1998—Hunter's staying over at Grandpa and Grandma's house tonight. He loves my parents, so I know he'll have fun.

He's doing a little better these days; no pneumonia right now—and that's always a good thing. But unfortunately he's been having really bad seizures. Dr. Duffner is trying to figure it all out. She might want Hunter to go on a medication that can only be purchased in Canada. We'll go anywhere for Hunter. If he needs it, we'll go get it because that's just the way it is.

Tonight is the final candle ribbon-tying in Attica for Hunter's Hope. The volunteers will be tying hunter green ribbons around thousands of baby-powder-scented taper candles. Knowing that people care and want to help us in any way they can is so encouraging. I can't wait to see the sea of candles light up the sky at Hunter's Day of Hope for Children. What a beautiful way to celebrate the incredible gift God has given us—our kids. That's one thing Jim and I share every time we have the opportunity to talk about our story. We want people to appreciate the gift of life because you never know what tomorrow holds. It's amazing what this disease has done to our family.

My mom's taking Hunter to Wayne's World for the candle-tying so everyone can meet him. She wants people to understand why we're fighting for the kids. They need to know.

December 23, 1998—Erin and Hunter had doctors' appointments today. They found blood and small crystals in Hunter's urine and think he might have kidney stones. You've got to be kidding me. As if he doesn't already have enough to deal with, now this. God, if You're listening, please help Hunter…he needs You. We all need You.

What a whirlwind year two was.

Hope was renewed when we started Hunter's Hope and our little buddy continued to battle so courageously. Because of Hunter's passion for life, we stopped treating him as if he was dying, and as a result we all started living... really living. Regardless of his daily struggles, Hunter's inner joy continued to radiate and penetrate the hearts of all who met him. It seemed as though even though the disease progressed, our hopes and Hunter's zest for life somehow overcame it all.

Chapter 9

Hunter at Three and Four

Year Three, 1999–2000

January 22, 1999 (Florida)—Thank God for water because Hunter loves it. He loves the pool, the ocean, and his Jacuzzi bath. Every day, at least once if not more, he's in the water. We've tried to take Hunter for a walk on the beach at least once a day, depending on how he's feeling. The warmer weather seems to do wonders for his overall health, especially his breathing. He's still on .50 liters of oxygen. What would we do without his oxygen?

Erin slept through the night all by herself last night. I'm so proud of her. She always wants to be with Hunter, but he's up most of the night so it's best for her to sleep in her own room. Is Erin getting what she needs? I hope so, because I'm doing my best. I wish I could be in two places at one time.

February 14, 1999—Happy birthday, Hunter and Jim...but not such a happy birthday—Hunter's in the hospital. It's

4:30 a.m. in the ICU and we need help. We need a miracle. Every time we come here I'm fearful I'll have to leave without Hunter in my arms.

God, please do something. Where are You? Am I not praying right? Please bring Hunter home. It's his birthday today and here we are in the hospital. Why? I don't understand Your ways but I'm trying to trust You in everything. But sometimes it's so hard, like right now. He's struggling. Lord, please intervene. Please!

April 8, 1999—Hunter went to the playground today. Grammie insists on taking Hunter to places I would never even think to take him, like the playground. Honestly, if she could safely put him on a roller coaster, she would. My mother would sit right alongside him, laughing with her hands in the air. I'm big and pregnant and have no ambition to do anything that requires a lot of energy.

This pregnancy has been the worst of all three by far. Thank God I have help. Reggie goes nonstop and takes such good care of everything, especially Hunter's things. She takes the time to iron all his sheets and little t-shirts. Hunter loves when she reads him stories because she's always so animated. He loves her back massages, too. I don't know how I'm going to take care of a baby, Hunter, and Erin. Lord, as always, I need You. Some things never change—clinging to You is one of them.

May 25, 1999—I don't know how Hunter does it. He puts up with so much all the time. Today in the bathtub I had to help him excrete two stones the size of small Grape Nuts cereal. Are you kidding me? Jim saw them and just about fainted. What's even crazier is the fact that Hunter didn't *even cry when they came out. How can that be? He's so tough.*

God, please continue to strengthen and heal Hunter's body. He needs rest and peace. Hunter is a constant reminder of our need for You.

June 24, 1999—Happy birthday, Camryn Lynn Kelly: 8 pounds, 7 ounces, 21¼ inches long—5:09 a.m. Welcome to the team, little rookie.

August 20, 1999—Hunter went to the dentist today to get his teeth cleaned. His teeth are so nice and straight and cute. Oddly, we love taking him, probably because he always shows off. (Of course, my mom took a bunch of pictures.) The dentist even commented on how amazed he was that Hunter appeared to understand exactly what he was saying. When he told Hunter to open his mouth a little wider, he did.

It's no surprise to us. We know that HB is fully cognitive. He understands exactly what's going on, but his body doesn't get the messages his brain is trying to communicate. He's such a smart kid. I'm really thankful that people like our dentist get to see that Hunter really does know what's going on.

I'm so busy now with the baby that I'm always exhausted, and Hunter hasn't been sleeping very much lately, so that's been really hard. I know we'll be okay, though. We have to press on and trust God in the midst of all this craziness. One day at a time, one hour at a time, one prayer at a time...

September 1, 1999—Lord, please help Hunter. He's been struggling with jumpy arms and seizures for two days

straight and nothing seems to help. It kills me to watch
him go through all this. I want to scream. But I have to be
strong and calm for Hunter's sake. I have to keep it together
for him.

Lord, hold me together. Please give me the strength I
need to take care of all three of my children. I can't do this
without Your help....

December 3, 1999 (My brother Jack and his wife, Kim's,
wedding)—Hunter looked incredibly handsome today. I'm so
thankful that Jack asked him to be a groomsman. He made
the wedding that much more wonderful.

I was amazed that he didn't need any suctioning during his part of the ceremony. He's so smart and knows just
when to keep it all in. His cute little tuxedo fit just right, and
he wore it with great pride for his uncle. Erin was a beautiful
flower girl, too. What a great day.

Hunter will be three years old in a few months—what a
miracle. He continues to astound all of us with his courage
and will to persevere. His life is a living testimony to the
grace and mercy of God. Thank You, Jesus.

December 23, 1999—The Christmas tree is up and looks
beautiful. Erin and Hunter helped decorate this year. Jim
threw some tinsel on the tree as he walked by (just kidding).
Tinsel is his favorite decoration but I can't stand it. At least
he doesn't try stringing a bunch of footballs around the tree.

Elizabeth got HB up in his stander for 30 minutes today
and he loved it. I loved the look on his face as he gazed at
the twinkle lights and colorful bulbs on the tree. The simple
things mean so much to Hunter. Standing up for 30 minutes
is a big deal. Breathing without apnea and secretions is a

big deal. Life itself is the greatest gift to him. He has taught us so much. I can't believe how shallow my life and existence were before Hunter. He makes life worth living. As difficult and heartbreaking as it is to see my son suffer, watching him enjoy every ounce of life is truly indescribable. Wow....

As Hunter continued to grow, so did our family with the addition of Camryn. There was never a dull moment for the Kelly family, and although Hunter needed constant care, the girls were just as demanding of my attention. I often felt torn between spending time with the girls and taking care of Hunter. However, God started to intervene in miraculous ways.

————

Year Four, 2000–2001

January 13, 2000 (Florida)—Grammie held Hunter close to the ocean waves, and when they rushed in and touched his cute little toes, he pulled his legs back. It was amazing. Just to see him move his legs like that all by himself was such a treat.

Erin had fun building sandcastles and making Hunter's feet disappear under mounds of sand. He seems more at peace by the ocean than anywhere else. I think he enjoys the sound of the waves and the warmth of the sun. Although he continues to have seizures, they don't last too long and then he seems fine. These fleeting moments of contentment when Hunter is doing well are priceless.

February 15, 2000 (Florida)—Hunter had a new feeding tube put in today. He went from a GT [gastrojejunal] to a JG [jejunostomy] tube. This tube will allow formula to go directly into his intestines rather than his stomach.

We changed his tube because he was getting pneumonia often and the doctors in Florida think he'll get it much less with the JG. I hope so. His poor little lungs have taken such a beating from all the aspirating. To think that we would know and understand all this feeding tube stuff is crazy. And yet I'm so thankful for all of it—for the suction machine, the feeding pump, and the oxygen—all of it. Everything we have to help Hunter is a gift—everything. He's a gift!

March 20, 2000 (Florida)—What a horrible day. Hunter's JG tube slipped out, so we had to rush him to the hospital. The doctor, who we don't even know, kept trying to thread the tube back in. I held Hunter's hand the entire time and we ended up being there for four hours. I want to scoop him up and run away. Watching Hunter suffer is excruciating when I can't do anything about it. Please help him, God. PLEASE!

April 28, 2000 (Attica, NY)—My mother is hysterical. She took Hunter to the Attica Library today and he got his own library card and checked out ten books. Then they strolled down Main Street and stopped at Wayne's World for some ice cream and then Busy Mart. I'm sure Grammie wanted to give Hunter a taste of her ice cream…my mom thinks Hunter should experience everything he physically can. I get that. I want him to be able to experience and taste certain foods too, but the risk is just too high because he can't swallow. Which means that if we didn't suction him in time, he might choke. It's just not worth the risk.

Still, I struggle with what to do. I shelter him as much as possible, but maybe he needs to be more exposed to the world around him. I have to let go, but it's hard…so hard.

Hunter went for a ride through the woods in the back of

Grandpa's tractor today, too. My mom said she wants to take Hunter to a shoe store tomorrow, to have him fitted for a new pair of sneakers. And then she and my aunt Dodie plan to take the kids to a farm so they can pet some animals. My mom is amazing. She loves taking Hunter on adventures she knows I would probably be reluctant to take him on.

June 3, 2000—We went to visit Bambi [Hunter's favorite horse] today. Hunter loves her so much. Of course I forgot to bring carrots...again.

Hunter was also up in his stander today playing the piano. When he gets his arms moving you can tell he's really trying to play the keys. Believe it or not, the music he makes actually sounds good—really good. I'm so proud of him. He tries so hard all the time and knows exactly what he's doing; he's a very smart kid.

He's still into Stuart Little, Little Bear, Davey and Goliath, and Franklin the Turtle. I love when all three of the kids fall asleep next to each other while watching a movie together. They're beautiful. Erin and Camryn love their brother and always see past his disease. I'm so blessed.

August 1, 2000—Crazy day; so much going on. Hunter had to get a CAT scan (computerized axial tomography) and an EEG (electroencephalogram) at Children's Hospital. Hunter's temperature has been all over the place lately—anywhere from 104.4 to 99.4—and he's been having more apnea and seizures. Please help him to breathe, Lord.

It's been so beautiful outside lately that we've tried to take Hunter out for a stroll as much as possible. When we're walking through the neighborhood, I find myself talking to him about the color of the sky, the grass, birds, and squirrels—things I never really paid much attention to in the past. He makes me so much more aware of everything. Lord, thank You for opening up my eyes through Hunter's. God, please heal my boy.

November 12, 2000—Dear Hunter... It's amazing how fast time goes by. We have been so busy that I haven't even had a chance until now to reflect on all the fun and exciting things you've been up to lately. Being a three-year-old boy is pretty cool, especially when you're a preschooler. Along with your awesome physical and occupational therapies, you are now a schoolboy.

Ms. Marion and Ms. Kristin have joined our team and they are so much fun. They have introduced you to a lot of neat things to help you learn more about yourself and the world around you. You've been experimenting a lot lately with different smells and surface textures. One of your favorite sessions was playing in the banana shaving foam. I had fun, too, especially watching you. You've been able to experience a lot of new and different things like pumpkin carving, leaf collecting, and horseback riding on Bambi.

You are getting so tall, Hunter. I'm amazed at how much you've grown. That little baby with the chunky-cheek face has grown into such a handsome boy. Erin and Camryn have so much fun with you. Camryn just wants to kiss and hug you all the time. We think she's going to be your next nurse because she's always trying to suction you and give you chest therapy. Erin loves to read to you and play Noah's ark. You are always so happy and excited whenever your two sisters are around. I also love watching my two favorite boys hang out together. To see your face whenever Daddy holds you is so special. He loves you so much.

Some days, Hunter, you are on the go so much that I just can't wait for bedtime. Although I love our Jacuzzi and playtime, I look forward to bedtime. There is nothing sweeter than getting all snuggly with you and holding your hand as we both drift off to sleep.

I love you so much, Hunter. What an immeasurable treasure from God you are. Each and every day that goes by with you by my side is a shower of blessings sent from heaven. Thank you for bringing so much love and joy into my life. I'm so proud to be your mom. Through all your suffering and struggles you continue to show such strength and courage. I will continue to pray that someday we will be holding hands and giggling while we run through a beautiful meadow chasing butterflies. If not here, then for eternity. I can't wait. I love you, little buddy.

Despite the birth of our daughter Camryn, and our joy at having another child, our marriage was fading into nothingness behind the scenes. Hunter, however, continued to grow and fearlessly fight the war being waged against him. Though outwardly it appeared that Hunter was wasting away, his inward spirit continued to shine ever so brightly as he battled seizures and all sorts of serious physical complications. His unbridled will to live filled our home and hearts with a joy beyond description.

And in the midst of everything I passionately pursued the heart of God. Hunter's struggles drove me to my knees—and God, in His mercy, kept me there. The more Krabbe disease tried to steal, the more life God poured into our family. Miracles were happening almost daily, none more significant than the realization that we all needed Jesus as our quarterback.

Chapter 10

Hunter at Five and Six

Year Five, 2001–2002

My journals start to read more like prayers now. My thoughts are so intertwined with prayer that it's hard to determine the difference . . . and I guess that's okay.

January 11, 2001—Days go by so fast, I can barely keep up with the daily demands, much less journal. Hunter has been so busy doing all sorts of fun activities with Team Hunter. Since he can't move his arms to play, Kristin taught HB how to use his breathing instead. At their latest session, she brought some colorful feathers and placed them close enough to Hunter that he could move them ever so slightly by breathing. Amazing. I could tell by the look on Hunter's face that he understood that he was the one moving the feathers. Those fleeting moments of independence mean so much to him. They mean the world to me too.

Hunter made a delicious chocolate chip cake with Elizabeth and Marion the other day. He got very messy but I could tell he was having a blast. I guess we're into baking lately because Grammie had Hunter frosting cookies, too. He's not the only one that gets all messy—it's always a team effort.

While Hunter gets a lot of exercise throughout the day, I think he enjoys the movement involved with baking or creating artwork. He doesn't mind hand-over-hand help. In fact, he welcomes the creative activities so much that I don't even think it bothers him that he's not the one moving. As long as his limbs are active, his body can relax some and he can play.

Today, my cousin Justin played the guitar for all of us. He's musically gifted and loves to share his talent and time with HB.

We're concerned about Hunter's hips, so we've scheduled an x-ray to get a better look at them. When we exercise his legs lately, you can feel his body resist. It's much easier to move his legs in the water, but he can't be in the bath all the time. Hopefully it's nothing serious. He needs his exercise.

February 15, 2001—We spent a lot of time opening Hunter's birthday presents today; actually, Camryn opened most of the gifts for her brother. That's what little sisters do.

Hunter was fitted for "the Vest" today. [The Vest Airway Clearance System is a medical device that helped Hunter to manage and mobilize secretions in his airway. Most children with cystic fibrosis use the vest.] I was nervous and insisted on trying it out first. Although I didn't really like how it felt on me, Hunter seemed to enjoy it. Besides, it will help his lungs and make chest therapy way more effective.

We have so much to be thankful for. My pumpkin boy is four years old! How can that be? Lord, You're so good to us, so good.

March 20, 2001—Okay, I don't know what it is with boys and cars, but they obviously go together. Hunter was up in his stander today and could have spent the entire day pushing his little cars down the makeshift ramp we made. He was fascinated with his ability to make the cars move all on his own.

Such simple little things bring him joy. A life so simple and yet so intense and complicated. Simplicity motivates him to live; yet complexity sustains his living. This concept is ironic. Lord, he needs what only You can give him: comfort in the midst of suffering, peace in the midst of chaos, and an undeniable hope that cultivates extraordinary courage. Please relax Hunter—his muscles are so tight and his little body is rigid...he needs to loosen up so he can play.

April 12, 2001 (Orlando, Florida—Disney Trip)—Thank You for getting us through our Disney trip. What a disappointment...except for the private dinner with Mickey Mouse. Big deal.

Sorry, it's just that we had high expectations for this trip and Hunter had such a difficult time. Thank You for the struggles and heartaches that keep us focused on our constant need for You. Help me to remember that You are in control, especially when things don't work out the way we had planned.

June 5, 2001—Hunter's been struggling a lot lately. He's been awake all night wrestling with secretions because of reflux, apnea, and nasty seizures. There's also a lot of blood in his stomach, especially during and after chest therapy.

Please give me strength to keep going. When will it end? Every morning upon awakening, I am confronted by a new set of circumstances to deal with. My baby is growing worse each day, just like the doctors said. Friends, family, and even perfect strangers all storm the throne of God with tear-filled prayers for him to be healed; yet he continues to worsen. When will he be released from this?

Sometimes I wish You would take Hunter. I hate when I feel that way! Please help me to be a better mother. I feel as though I live in a combat zone and I'm constantly battling this invading army that is trying to take down my family. Nightmares of being ambushed by hostile forces plague me. I sleep, but get no rest. This is my life.

September 9, 2001—The only birthday present I want is healing for Hunter. Is that too much to ask, Lord? Who am I to question what is beyond my comprehension? I can't help it; this is so hard. When I don't understand, please help me to trust that You are in control.

I think if my mother had it her way, Hunter would move in with her. They're so cute together. Rescue Heroes, Playdoh, Lite Brite, and magnets are a big hit lately…Oh, and baking continues to be a common adventure around here. I suppose it wouldn't hurt if I learned how to cook…Nope, don't have time…ha, ha.

October 31, 2001 (Halloween)—Hunter dressed up as Franklin the Turtle. I can't believe I found just the right pieces to make his costume. He's adorable.

November 17, 2001 (Ralph Wilson Stadium, Wall of Fame)—I don't know if I can describe the thrilling moments our family experienced today at the Buffalo Bills Wall of Fame ceremony. It was so exciting! Just thinking about it makes me cry.

Our entire family, decked out in number 12 jerseys, headed over to the stadium in typical Kelly game-day fashion: by motor home. Much preparation was needed in order to get Hunter and the girls ready to walk out onto the football field. The deafening roar of 80,000 wild Bills fans was exhilarating. I was so excited for Hunter I could hardly contain myself.

What an honor for Jim's number to be retired and his name to go up on the stadium wall. What an even greater blessing to have Hunter there to experience it with his daddy. Unbelievable! God, You are so good.

December 10, 2001—Hunter weighs 28 pounds and he's getting so tall.

Christmas is approaching, so there's been a lot of holiday activity going on around the house. Tammy [Hunter's nurse] says that whenever she and Hunter play a board game together, he always wins. She doesn't let him win, he just does. He's so cool. We made a gingerbread house the other day, played with snow, and painted some really cool tree ornaments.

Hunter loves any activity where he can get all messy—typical boy. Camryn hounds Hunter continuously so she can join in on whatever he's doing. She is the sweetest little sister. They love each other so much. Whenever Erin and Camryn snuggle or play with Hunter, there is a look of contentment on his face that is unmistakable. I can only imagine what he's thinking or what he might want to say to them. It's so hard to describe, but I can see love all over my boy. He's happy. Despite everything he must endure, he's happy to be here; to be alive; to be near his sisters. In return, their brother has taught the girls the meaning of unconditional

*love by letting them experience it long before they were old
enough to understand its literal significance.*

*Hunter has a fresh haircut for Christmas. He's gorgeous.
Lord, I hope this doesn't sound weird but I feel like I see You
in Hunter's eyes, looking into me.*

As time went by and Hunter continued to grow and battle
Krabbe disease, we became even more committed to providing
every opportunity available for him to live the life God gave
him. In my quest to draw near to the heart of the Father, I found
myself able to surrender to Him in increasing measure. This
allowed me to enjoy Hunter and life even more.

Despite the crazy, roller-coaster life we were living and the
disease trying to destroy my son, there was more laughter, fun,
and joy in our home than ever before. Somehow our home was
filled with life—and even my dying marriage couldn't prevent it.
Maybe because I was more focused on Hunter and his life than on
anything that concerned Jim and our marriage.... It was as if the
love enveloping our family, in some indescribable way, allowed us
to experience a peace and joy beyond our circumstances.

Don't get me wrong—tears were shed and the fear of losing
Hunter continued to haunt me, but the abundant life that poured
out of my desperately sick son transformed our home, and it was
good...really good.

———

Year Six, 2002–2003

*February 7, 2002 (Children's Hospital of Buffalo)—Lord, You
knew every detail about this day before it came to be. As I
sit here in the ICU and look at Hunter hooked up to all these
machines, it's undeniable—he's beautiful. Thank You for the*

striking beauty and relentless strength I see in my son right now. His determination and desperation to live are honorable for such a little boy. Lord, how blessed I am that You gave him to me, to our family. Please keep him from pain. I'm terrified of losing him, and You know it. I don't want to let him go. Do I have to? Is today the day? I believe that Your timing is perfect. Help me with my unbelief.

When I'm fearful, please help me to persevere by faith. When my faith weakens, please God, hold me up for him. He cannot see me curled up in a ball on the floor, crying (like my body and mind are screaming at me to do). My heart is urging me with a still, small voice to stand up, look into Hunter's eyes, and tell him it's okay. It's all going to be okay no matter what happens today. I know this is You, Lord; You who dwell in my heart and spirit, consoling me, inspiring me, and giving me strength. Nevertheless, the constant battle between flesh and spirit is intense and demanding.

Please fill our hearts and minds with a peace that surpasses all understanding. Thank You for Hunter, his incredible life, and all that You have taught us through him. When I wrestle with why You allow Hunter to struggle so much, please remind me that You will never abandon him. He is always on Your mind, always.

Hasn't he suffered enough? Forgive me, Father, but it rips my heart to shreds when I see him lying here so weak and fragile, struggling to breathe. Rescue him, please, Lord…thank You.

April 19, 2002—Like father, like son. HB was so engrossed in the football and hunting videos he watched today with his daddy. At first I was very apprehensive about letting him watch hunting, but Jim insisted. Go figure.

Hunter loves watching his daddy play football. Even though the videos are of past Buffalo Bills games, Jim still gets riled up and Hunter loves all the hooting and hollering. I try not to interrupt the boys whenever they hang out because Jim doesn't stay put for very long. His constant coming and going drives me nuts. I need more patience—but as Jim would say, "But I'm not a doctor, so why do I need more patients?" Very funny. Too bad I'm not laughing.

We live under the same roof but we are worlds apart. What a shame. I don't have the time or energy to focus on anything other than the kids, especially Hunter.

May 4, 2002 (Erin's Seventh Birthday Party)—As usual we went overboard for Erin's birthday. My mom bravely strolled Hunter outside, where kids were running around everywhere. Thankfully, Hunter and all his medical paraphernalia don't intimidate Erin's friends. They're intrigued and curious but not fearful. My cousin Jessica face-painted a horse on Hunter's cheek. I try not to think about it too much, but I can't help but wonder if he feels bad that he can't run around like other kids. He can see them and he knows what they're doing. Lord, please heal my boy....

June 24, 2002—We went to visit Bambi and her new foal, Ohmeister (I'm not sure of the spelling). What a great day at the barn. Bambi is so calm around Hunter, thank God. Ohmeister is a frisky little thing, and for some reason she liked my boots.

Hunter went fishing yesterday and caught ten fish. It wasn't easy, but once we got him up in his stander, all we had to do was throw the line in. The fish were biting like crazy so it didn't take long for Hunter to catch one, and then another, and yet another…a professional angler all in one day.

As soon as the bobber went under we all started jumping up and down with excitement. It's a good thing my aunt Dodie knows how to hook a worm and release a fish. She's so much fun to be around, and the kids love her. She has really fun ideas that usually involve animals, nature, and making weird faces. What a blessing she is.

July 16, 2002—Hunter lost his second tooth today, the lower-right front one. It's a big deal…do you hear me? He's alive and he lost a tooth and he wasn't even supposed to be breathing and living right now! Glory to God!

Hunter bowls, swims, and plays baseball—maybe not like all the other boys his age, but he does it nonetheless. He's an extraordinary little kid with so much love, it pours out of him in buckets. And he's Yours, Lord; he's Your boy now and always. Even in the shadow of doubt, I know this to be true—my boy belongs to You. He's covered in the strength of Your grace and the radiance of Your glory. I feel Your light wrap around our family even in great darkness. Please flood our lives with love and hope that eclipses what we know right now.

Play the piano and shake the tambourine and bells, little Hunter, because all of heaven is listening…we're all listening…and you play the most beautiful music I've ever heard.

August 4, 2002 (Canton, Ohio—NFL Hall of Fame)—I cannot believe how incredible the last few days have been. The hoopla surrounding induction weekend is over the top. Jim is so excited, as he should be. He made it, and he deserves to be here right now receiving this high honor. Thank You for sustaining us and for strengthening Hunter so he could be present to watch and listen to his daddy's induction. Every moment was special.

Jim's speech was by far the most memorable, all because of Hunter. [You can read his speech in Appendix E, but it won't compare to hearing it in person—especially the part directed toward Hunterboy.] Our son's plight set Jim's powerful words far above the rest.

It's amazing my little buddy was able to endure the commotion, certainly a tribute of love for his daddy. I could tell he was so excited to be a part of this monumental honor. He made it through the entire ceremony—as sweltering hot as it was, he did it. We were all so proud. Yet, even in the midst of such a wonderful blessing, heaviness swept over my heart...Why Hunter? Why our son?

Just when I feel completely overwhelmed, You show me You're right here. As I glance outside our hotel window, about 200 yards away, there—elevated above all the other buildings—a yellow cross graces the sky, soothing my pain and filling my heart with hope again, even if just for now. Thank You, Jesus! You're the only one who understands. Because of You, I have hope.

October 8, 2002—Erin Marie writes "Trust Jesus" all over the place—on Hunter's schedule book, all over my journals, on tiny pieces of paper scattered throughout the house. I need her reminders. I need to trust You. Sometimes it's hard, like right now, when Hunter continues to struggle with apnea and seizures. Both of his hips are bothering him, too, and even though the brace seems to help, he appears to be very uncomfortable.

He can't tell me where it hurts; he has never been able to

tell his mommy where it hurts. My mind wanders and I think of little boys on the playground scraping their knee, or on a baseball diamond sliding into home plate and getting all scratched up. The first thing they do is run to their mommy for a kiss and a few comforting words. My baby has excruciating pain—pain that worsens every day—and he cannot tell me a word. He can't tell me where to kiss. Just once, I wish he could. I need him to be able to tell me so I can do something about it.

Please eradicate this wretched disease that has come to steal, kill, and destroy the precious life of my son. Make a way, Lord, please. Do You hear me? Do You see him suffering? How long will You wait to lift the burden? How long? Until that day, we can't survive without You...please help us.

October 31, 2002 (Halloween)—Hunter dressed up as Stuart Little.

December 17, 2002—Every time I read The Three Trees to the kids, I cry. That book speaks right to my fear and doubt. There is a purpose for our trials that goes beyond my ability to grasp, and I've just got to let go and...let God.

Hunter's eyes have been bothering him a lot lately so we've been putting eye drops in often. He is incredibly patient with all the poking and prodding we do to his body.

Thank You for Hunter and for getting our attention through his precious life. You know what it's like to watch Your Son suffer—Lord, have mercy on us, please. Hunter needs You. He's so tough, but he's getting tired. It's so hard to watch him struggle. Don't give up, little buddy; please don't give up.

Even now, after typing in the previous entry, that same wave of worry swept over me and I remember how desperate I was for Hunter to be free from pain and bodily strife. Surrendering my fears was a daily battle that I sometimes failed to conquer.

As you can imagine, Jim's Hall of Fame induction was the highlight of 2002 for our entire family. I'll never forget the stillness of the crowd when Jim thanked God for Hunter, and the eruption of cheers after he said, "My hero, my soldier, my son, Hunter. I love you, buddy." I'm certain that Jim's speech will be considered one of the best induction speeches of all time, all because of Hunter.

We were so thankful that Hunter was able to be there. Although Jim Kelly's enshrinement in the Hall of Fame that day was a grand honor, Jim and I both agree that nothing compares to our son taking his place in the "Hall of Faith."

Chapter 11

Hunter at Seven

Year Seven, 2003–2004

As you'll see, my journals become more and more focused on God at this time rather than on Hunter and the girls. Also, I pray more fervently for my husband. I suppose at some point the realization that Hunter was going to be healed eventually, no matter what (either here on Earth or in heaven), gave me an invincible peace and comfort that allowed me to pray more for Jim, whose "illness" was rooted in his soul rather than his body.

His was an issue of the heart, a healing only God could grant. If the heart is the wellspring of life, then I was willing to get down on both knees for his.

January 23, 2003—I'm laughing right now because my aunt Dodie is hysterical. She had Hunter rummaging through our kitchen cupboards today while he was up in his Kid Kart. Despite his apnea and bowel issues, he still wants to have fun. He doesn't have that much free time during the day because of his jam-packed therapy schedule and school session, so we try to get in at least a few hours of kid fun. He was also messing around in his closet and pulling clothes and stuff out of his armoire drawers. As I write, I can't help laughing, especially because I'm such a neat freak. He had things spread out all over his closet and the kitchen. I'm certain that if the two of them were able, they would have been throwing things around the kitchen as well.

We'll be taking Hunter to the hospital tomorrow for a chest and hip x-ray, ECHO [echocardiogram] test, and sputum culture, per Dr. Duffner. She's such a blessing. Hunter's 42 inches tall now and growing; thank You, Lord.

February 23, 2003—Erin asked me to pray over her and kiss her while she sleeps tonight. She knows Hunter and I are up throughout the night, and certainly I will pray.

Jim and Hunter played a football game on the computer today. It's odd, but I feel like whenever Hunter is with his daddy, there's almost an atmosphere of love around them. An aura of protection and love enveloping them. When I observe this happening, it's almost as though Hunter's love for Jim is so profound that it mirrors God's love for us.

I see this in my son. I see his Christlike qualities and am not ashamed to admit it. There is only one Jesus Christ, and I know this; it's just that my son is getting closer to Christ every day. Hunter takes on His attributes. The attribute that seems the strongest is his ability to show love without speaking, without writing us notes, without running to us and throwing his arms around us. I see his unconditional love for his father and you can observe the peace on Jim's face when they are together. This is a beautiful image. If only I could capture it in my mind forever.

I sure wish I loved Jim the way HB does. What I wouldn't do for some of that love. I know it comes from Your heart, Lord, so please fill mine. Please love him through me. I can't do it—please change me; change the way I feel and how I treat my husband.

The greatest thing about Jim is that he keeps me seeking You. Please make a way! Show me how to love my husband the way Hunter does, the way You do. I thirst for Your patience, Your forgiveness, Your understanding, and Your humility.... I want to love my husband this way, I just don't know how. To me it looks hopeless and helpless. I think Jim needs You more than Hunter does.

March 18, 2003 (Children's Hospital)—Heavenly Father, at times like these I selfishly long for Hunter to be with You in heaven, far away from emergency rooms, needles that prick, machines that beep... everything about this place. Help me to live each day with one foot in eternity and the other planted soundly on this earth. Grounded enough to be a great mother, wife, friend, daughter, and disciple.

They're telling us Hunter's starting to lose his "involuntary blink"—the kind that we all do without thinking. This is causing him to have serious eye issues. Come on, please, God; You know he blinks once for yes. If he also loses his voluntary blink, then what? Please don't take that from him, too! That's how he talks. That's how he says "I love you."

The whole concept of Hunter being here [at Children's Hospital] for some greater purpose tests my faith to the extreme. My heart knows God has a plan and is in control. Nevertheless, my mind cannot stop intruding on my faith and questioning, what purpose can this serve? PLEASE

TELL ME! How can this be good? Make him better now, please!!!

Whoa—I'm yelling at God. Jill, get a grip. Lord, forgive me and remind me of Your sovereignty and perfect will. Please make Hunter well so he can go home and play with his sisters, snuggle, take a warm bath—all the things he loves to do. He's so brave. I'm still hopeful that You might consider healing Hunter—totally, this side of heaven—but Your ways are higher and better than mine. Help me to take care of the girls and Hunter. Please impart Your supernatural strength into my life.

April 16, 2003—Mrs. Basinski [Erin's kindergarten teacher] came over for a visit today. She brought a beautiful black-and-white rabbit with her, and the kids enjoyed the little cuddly critter. She also read some wonderful Easter books. She's a wonderful friend and great teacher.

Although it's not my favorite medical apparatus, the CoughAssist [a mechanical device used to clear bronchial secretions] appears to be helping Hunter. Imagine that, a machine that helps you cough. As his body continues to deteriorate, I hope there's always something—a machine and medicine, anything—to help him battle this wretched disease.

I haven't been able to write as often lately; we've been too busy and I'm completely exhausted. A recent huge blessing: Hunter was exercising his arms, moving them up and down, all by himself. Watching him try so hard and move on his own is a miracle. Do miracles always have to be huge, earth-shattering events? Please assure me that all the little hurdles Hunter achieves can be deemed as miracles. Lord, what about the little things that are profound and life-changing?

Dear Reader, will you please do something for me? Will you look up the definition of *miracle*? (Seriously, grab your dictionary, go to the "m" section, and read what it says.) Our son Hunter fit every description.

The Webster's dictionary that I'm looking at right now says that a miracle is: "(1) an event or action that apparently contradicts known scientific laws and is hence thought to be due to supernatural causes, esp. to an act of God; (2) a remarkable event or thing; marvel; (3) a wonderful example."[1] Hunter's life "contradicted all known medical laws." (I know it says "scientific," but just go with me here.) The doctors stopped trying to figure him out because he didn't fit the Krabbe model found in their textbooks. He was supposed to die before his second birthday, but he didn't. According to the definition, I would consider that "a remarkable event to marvel over," and certainly "a wonderful example."

His life was a constant example of courage, suffering, joy, and so much more. And if I can be so bold, he was the miracle. I know the miracles in the Bible were different from what I'm talking about, but can't God speak a miracle through a little boy, without words? I know that the God I worship can work miracles even now through my son.

Let's go back to the journal entries....

May 18, 2003—Today is my wedding anniversary. Yippee (yeah, right). Jim and I have been married seven years. Am I supposed to be happy about that?

Lord, You saw that Leah [a woman in the Old Testament book of Genesis] was unloved. You looked on her affliction. You listened to her cries and remembered her sorrow. I know that You see me! I know that You see my marriage.

I feel like an old woman, like a dried-up lake, like a shriveled flower—my soul feels withered and numb. I'm lonely and afraid. Please soften my heart and change me. My desires are dead—is this because of my unwillingness to fully forgive? I'm so tired and have no energy to even try. Please rescue me from myself and from this lonely road I am traveling. Replace bitterness with beauty, sadness with a promise of love, and dread with a yearning for intimacy. I want to give up—I sort of already have...and yet this beautiful boy lying here next to me is a constant reminder to press on, to never give up—not on anything or anyone, especially his daddy.

May 29, 2003—Hunter was checking himself out in the mirror today because he lost another adorable baby tooth. I hate to see his baby teeth go because they're so perfect, but he's growing and big boy teeth are coming in...and that's awesome. As I sit here writing, I'm overcome by the simplicity of my son's life, and yet the magnitude of suffering he endures is far from simple.

I think HB has looked at himself in a mirror maybe a dozen times in his entire life. Unfortunately, and I hate to admit it, I spend way too much time in front of a mirror. There must be something incredibly profound in this mirror thing.

Hunter's free from the expectations of the mirror. That's it. And quite possibly that's why he radiates such beauty all the time. His cares are not of this world. Amazing, so amazing.

June 2, 2003—Hunter has a broken arm. I can't believe this. As hard as we try and as careful as we are, somehow he broke his arm. The fracture is right below his shoulder.

We're all shocked. He was having a hard time yesterday with apnea, probably because of his arm. As if he doesn't have enough to deal with, now this. How did this happen?

The doctors are thinking he might need more calcium and magnesium in his diet to strengthen his bone density, especially because he's sedentary and doesn't move on his own. Please help him. Even though he has a broken arm, we're still planning on flying a kite tomorrow. When will the tears cease?

July 18, 2003—After a trip to the hospital today and a few more x-rays, it looks like Hunter's arm has finally healed. Thank God!

We had so much fun dancing around in the pool the other day. All three kids were piled on top of me and I was afraid Hunter's oxygen tank was going to fall in the water. Thankfully, it didn't.

Hunter's getting longer and heavier but I can still carry him. I'd carry him even if I couldn't. If I could pack him in a backpack and take him everywhere with me, I would. I can't get enough of that incredible kid.

August 28, 2003—What a whirlwind the last four days have been. Mark Schultz [a Christian recording artist] was in town for the Buffalo Bills game and he came over and performed a few songs for us. Our favorite is "He's My Son." As usual, we were crying.

A few days ago Hunter went horseback riding on Bambi out at Aunt Chris's barn. He also went fishing and stopped over at Aunt Dodie's house to visit her pet bird, Quaker, and her dog, Peanut. I think Hunter liked Quaker, especially when he started talking.

We've discovered that Ellen [Hunter's nurse] loves taking pictures just as much as my mother and I do. She's already given me a few mini photo albums filled with pictures that captured moments I was unable to.

What a great gift photos are. I treasure photos of Hunter because in the back of my mind, I know they will comfort me and jog my memory when Hunter has left this earthly place. You can never have too many pictures, especially of Hunterboy. Every picture, even the bad ones (if there is such a thing)—all of them are precious reminders of Your faithfulness, Lord.

Hunter has another loose tooth. He's six years old. I can't believe it.

October 22, 2003—Robert [Hunter's best friend] came over today with his mom. This is their second play date this month, and he's coming over on Halloween, too. Hunter loves being with his best friend more than he enjoys being with anyone else. I'm speechless when it comes to those two boys. When they get together it's as if the entire world around them vanishes and they're the only two people in the world.

Robert has introduced Hunter to the kind of silly boy stuff I would've never even considered for him, like mismatched socks, gooey bugs, silver astronaut blankets and space food, Bionicles and erupting volcanoes (oops, I think Jaden, my cousin Jessica's son, introduced HB to volcanoes)—all sorts of adventurous fun. What an unprecedented friendship. I've never witnessed anything like it.

You have done immeasurably more than we could've ever asked or imagined through their friendship. Thank You for Robert and his mother, Elizabeth. They are amazing people.

I never thought Hunter would experience the blessing of a best friend, but he has, and I can't thank You enough.

November 3, 2003 (Children's Hospital)—Leg x-rays and a full cast put on. Why, God—why? Doesn't Hunter already have enough to deal with? Now he has a broken femur. What in the world is going on?

I'm not going to let anyone touch him ever again. Two major bones broken in the last six months. This is ridiculous. How's he going to take a bath with a cast on? All this suffering is making me sick.

I know I should be thankful that he's still here, but I'm so drained from all this brokenness in his body and in my heart. It's not about me—I get that. It's not even about Hunter; it's about Your glory and will. Not having an answer to my nagging doubts drives me crazy. Father, I need Your lap and Your loving arms wrapped around me. Hunter needs You.

On December 13, 2003, Hunter was taken by ambulance to Children's Hospital. On the fifteenth, Hunter was put on a ventilator. At approximately 4:00 a.m. on the sixteenth, as I journaled the desperation of my soul like never before, a certain peace came over me and I was confident Hunter would make it home one more time. It was then that I began to think back on the extraordinary chain of events that had brought our family to this moment—the events you have just read about.

I'm convinced that the peace I felt and the assurance I had that Hunter would survive came from God; and indeed, despite his frailty and the evil downward spiral of Krabbe symptoms, Hunter's determined little body resisted surrender and the radiant light of his spirit was not snuffed out.

On December 21 at 11:20 a.m., the ventilator tube was taken

out and we made it home a few days later, just in time for Christmas. I wrote this letter to Hunter in the midst of everything:

Hunter, I'm so sorry that Mommy can't make you all better, little buddy. I will never fully understand why you must suffer so much. You're amazing, incredibly brave, and more handsome than any prince. Your irrepressible determination to beat this disease is astounding. I'm so proud of you.

I have asked God why. Why another broken bone? Why kidney stones? Why pneumonia and apnea all the time? I've asked Him for you, honey—so that maybe I would have an answer for you. I was in such a fog today wrestling with all your hardships, and what God reminded me of is this: You are here. You're alive, little buddy! I praise God for today. We have today and that's it. Thank you for being you, Hunter. The Lord is your shield and your hiding place. He will protect you and lead you home, soldier boy.

Chapter 12

Hunter at Eight

Year Eight, 2004–2005

Once again, my journal entries shift from recording memorable moments and prayers to simple love letters to Hunter. Most of my 2004 journals are filled with letters and vignettes to my son, as well as Scriptures and quotes that were significant during our journey.

After reading through my journals and Hunter's schedule books, I realized there was so much that had happened that I'd forgotten about. Since Hunter was no longer a toddler, he was able to experience a lot of different and exciting adventures. Young boy adventures I still can't believe we allowed him to participate in, like snowmobiling, sledding, and playing with reptiles. Hunter holding a twelve-foot yellow python and a baby alligator is not the safest activity, but I guess that's what boys do. And despite my misgivings, I felt blessed watching my son have so much fun.

February 1, 2004 (Hunter's Haven Lodge [Jim's hunting lodge located in Ellicottville, New York, on 150 acres of

God's country])—Maybe Mommy's a little crazy, or maybe
I love you like crazy and that's why I let you go sledding and
snowmobiling. It's amazing how things change. I was able to
let go of my fears so that you could enjoy some fantastic
winter fun.

Hunter, can you believe it? You did it! You actually went
snowmobiling. Daddy would've been so proud of you. I can't
wait to tell him all about it when he gets home from the
Super Bowl. Even though I'm a cautious snowmobile driver,
it's a good thing Grammie had a tight grip on you. Aunt
Dodie and Justin drove the four-wheeler so that your suction machine was always close, just in case you needed it,
but you did great. We were a sight to see. I could tell that
you were having so much fun, and even though she was a little nervous, I think Grammie had fun, too. I hope you weren't
cold, buddy. We bundled you up as much as we could without
turning you into an abominable snowman.

Hunter, the bunk-bed fort you built at the lodge was so
cool. I forgot the special password to get in, so you'll have
to tell me it again. Oh, and I think it's very exciting that you
know how to play pool now. You little pool shark. I don't even
know how to play, so you'll have to teach me. I love you, little
soldier—more than you know.

April 2, 2004—Every day you grow more handsome, Hunter.
I've never met anyone so beautiful. You're so tall (44½
inches) and getting heavier by the day, but I can still carry
you. Don't worry—I'll always carry you. I'll just find some
new apparatus so that I can carry my boy anywhere and
everywhere. If I have to I'll design it, and Grammie can make
it. We'll call it the Hunter Pack. Even when I'm old and gray,
I'll carry you. You are a light in our home that shines and

radiates with such brilliance. You are so fun to be around and take care of. We all love you so much.

And how about your best friend, Robert—isn't he a blessing? Your friendship is a priceless treasure, a gift from God. Every time the two of you get together it's an adventure. Robert always compliments you, telling you how handsome and wonderful you are. The other day he brought you a Bionicle (something you know Mommy knows very little about) and put it all together for you. You would watch him intently as he put each piece together. I saw excitement and anticipation light your eyes. You were smiling, weren't you? After Robert had everything assembled, you, Robert, and Daddy had a battle or whatever you boys call it. Watching you play with the two most important guys in your life is very special.

There's talk of you going to one of Robert's football games in September. That would be great. Please know how very much I love you, young man.

July 2, 2004—Dearest Hunter: We went on a golf cart ride today with nurse Ellen. You enjoyed cruising around our neighborhood. We had to be on the lookout for squirrels and chipmunks, didn't we? They were everywhere.

As I snuggle next to you and write this, it's 4:00 a.m. Mommy just finished doing your chest therapy and you're exhausted. Sleep, little buddy; you need your rest. God has blessed our family in so many ways through you, Hunter. What a remarkable way for God to express His love for us by creating you. Press on, soldier boy. Have I told you lately how much I love you? I never imagined my heart could ever love anyone as much as I love you and your sisters.

You are so smart. Do you remember that lady who came

to our house the other day to check your vision? First of all, buddy, I know you can see. Just because you're having a hard time blinking and closing your eyes doesn't mean you can't see. The lady was very impressed with your ability to track and follow directions. She thinks you would highly benefit from vision therapy at least once a week, so we're going to give it a try. I'm so thankful there are so many wonderful people who sincerely care and want to help you grow and prosper.

How about Ms. Susan, your teacher—isn't she great? She has lots of fun and exciting ideas. I'll never forget when she brought the life cycle of frogs over for class. I know you remember that day because that's when the frog peed all over her pants. As many times as you and Jericka [my cousin Jessica's daughter] have played with frogs, not one has ever peed on you, thank God. Ms. Susan was a good sport, wasn't she? We all laughed and laughed. Aren't you glad Mommy loves to take pictures, because we caught this one on film.

I want you to know how excited I am that you've been reading the Bible almost every single day. God has a lot of very important things to tell us, doesn't He? I love you, best boy ever—and Jesus loves you more…He does. His love is in you and we all see it…we all see Him through you. Thank you for being you!

August 30, 2004—Do you have any idea how much I love you? Hunter, I love you more than…

…the most stunning sunset to ever color the sky.

…the most beautiful butterfly God has ever created.

…my heart can handle.

…my favorite things.

...sleep.

...I can understand.

...my most memorable happenings.

...you will ever know,

...myself.

...all the world's most priceless treasures.

...anything.

...life itself.

...words can say.

September 9, 2004—Of all the gifts I'm most thankful for in this very moment, Lord Jesus, You're it. In this world with all its abundance, You are life to me. You are everything. You keep on giving; there is no end to Your grace and goodness. In You I am held together. Held together with a love that binds the parts of me that cannot function alone. If I rely on my brain, it will confuse me. If I rely on my body, I will fall apart. If I rely on other people, they will never meet my expectations. If I rely on my heart, it will bleed and break.

When I look to You, Lord, and rely on You, I am whole and I can live. I am able to think with my brain, stand on my feet, love people for how You created them to be, and possess a heart that beats for You and allows me to go on. I know You hold Hunter. You hold our entire family. Thank You for Hunter. We trust You with every breath he takes. You give and You take away.

October 31, 2004 (Halloween)—Hunter and Erin Marie dressed up as Spider-Man. Camryn was Strawberry Shortcake. I was hoping I could get Jim to dress up as a giant hamster, but he wouldn't go for it. He did his usual: a camouflaged hunter. It figures. No wonder our son's name is Hunter. I love that name.

Robert dressed up as Larry the Cucumber from Veggie-Tales and HB was supposed to be Bob the Tomato. How in the world was I supposed to make a tomato costume? Now that I'm thinking about it, I guess Hunter could have worn all red—his favorite color—but what fun is that? I think he was a great Spider-Man. I'm amazed that he tolerated the mask over his face, but he did. What a resilient little boy.

Jim was so sad the other day, and even though he didn't cry, I think he wanted to. He was talking about our nephew Zac, who's playing Little League football right now, and how he wishes Hunter could do the same. I often forget about his pain. Forgive me, Lord, and help me to see beyond my own anguish so that maybe somehow I can comfort Jim, even when I don't feel like it.

Please mend our broken hearts. We're sad that Hunter will never be able to fulfill all the hopes and dreams we once had for him. He'll never throw a touchdown pass to his cousin or storm the end zone for his team. He will do, and is accomplishing, so much more, I know, but these are the desires of a daddy's heart, and it's excruciating. Please, Lord, I haven't asked You in a while but it's heavy on my heart. Can You feel the weight of my heart pressing You to heal Hunter? Please heal him. Please heal all of us. Help us to never lose hope and forgive us for the times when we doubt You and all You can do. Help us to trust and believe that You have the better plan...always.

November 22, 2004—Hunter, here I go again. I know how much you love when Grammie and Mommy read these to you, so here's more for your precious little ears to hear and for your heart to receive.

I Love…

…when you, Erin, and Camryn snuggle up and watch a movie together.

…when you watch old football games with your daddy.

…when it's just you and me.

…how you endure.

…that you remind me to be tough whenever I don't feel so good.

…that you radiate God's glory.

…that I see Jesus in you.

…to hear the bubbles from your oxygen tank.

…when you have paint under your nails, because that's a sign that you did a fun art project. You're an artist. Mommy treasures all of your special creations.

…when Grammie sings to you in the Jacuzzi—especially when she sings "Soldier Boy." She's crazy about you, and you know it.

…when you lay across my lap and we just stare at each other.

…that your birthday is on Valentine's Day, your daddy's birthday and my favorite holiday—thanks, God.

…that people I don't even know write me letters to tell me how special you are. That's so cool.

…when people come up to me and tell me that they named their baby boy Hunter because of you. Isn't that great? People think you're something else, little buddy.

…that because of you, we formed the Hunter's Hope Foundation and lots of children's lives are being saved as a result of the amazing work God is doing there.

...that life is better because of you.

I love you, Hunter James Kelly.

I promise I'll write more, you cute little pumpkin boy.

Hunter loved it when my mother and I read my journals to him. Most of what I wrote was for me, for the sole purpose of reminding me of every single reason I loved Hunter as much as I did. I wanted to make sure not one of his qualities, expressions, or attributes was ever forgotten—regardless of how small they seemed at the time.

Initially, sharing my Hunter journals with Hunter never crossed my mind. My mother started reading them to him during the night, and he enjoyed them so much that she eventually made a video for him. The video was a collage of photos with soft background music and my mother doing the voice-over, reading my journal entries.

Our homemade videos were very unique. Because Hunter spent a lot of time lying sideways during chest therapy (which he had to have every four hours around the clock), my mother created DVDs that he could easily watch from that position. Everything on the DVD was sideways—perfect for Hunter's viewing pleasure.

The simplest change made such a huge difference.

December 17, 2004—Hunter, I can't believe how fast time goes by. In two months you'll be eight years old. How can that be? Despite the usual issues, you've been fairly healthy lately. Your eye-band [a special band my mother made to help Hunter close his eyes. He was unable to use the muscles around his eyes, so we had to figure out a way to help him close them] and gel have helped your eyes a lot. Grammie's so creative, isn't she? What will she think of next?

Hunter, I know your burdens are way more than you can handle. You are incredibly brave and strong and you never give up, but I want you to know that the Lord knows and He'll carry you through until you see Him face-to-face. Your life and breath are in His hands, and He knows when heaven needs you more than we do. Until that day, we're here for you and we'll do whatever it takes to provide for all of your needs. We'll do whatever it takes to kiss and snuggle you for as long as we can. We'll do whatever it takes through Hunter's Hope to help all the little boys and girls suffering from disease. We'll never give up, Hunter, never. Hang in there, little buddy. Don't give up.

Despite overwhelming odds and the devastation caused by Krabbe disease, Hunter was full of life. He gave himself away so unselfishly, and although life in our home revolved around his constant care, we were given immeasurably more than we gave. As odd as this may sound—and believe me, it's radical—I forgot that Hunter was dying from Krabbe disease.

I forgot.

He was living, and I believed he would keep on living.

The Last Seven Months, January–August 2005

These are the last few journal entries before Hunter met Jesus. Just as I never wanted to say good-bye to my boy, I don't want this to be my final set of journals—my last hopes, fears, prayers, and letters to my son. I don't want it to end. Not now, not ever.

Praise God it doesn't have to.

What I hold now are journals filled with memories that don't even compare to the real thing. I'll hold my boy again someday.

This I know for sure. Until I do, I'll keep these memories close, but I won't cling to them. Rather, I'm going to cling to the One who created my boy and made every minute with him possible. I'm going to cling to the One who provided a way for our entire family and all who knew and loved Hunter to see him again.

We'll see him again. Of this I am certain! This is my hope. The kind of hope that has no end.

February 14, 2005—Happy birthday, Hunter—you're eight years old. Your life is nothing short of a miracle, a gift from the hand of a good and merciful God.

Thank you for being so sweet and full of life. You make our home a place I long to be. Your eyes and face look especially bright today. I think you even got a little more handsome. How can that be? Today you are loved and cherished more than words can say and more than you will ever know.

Hunter, I pray that you will continue to shine for Jesus more and more with each passing day. I hope you will be free from worldly troubles and that you will always fix your eyes on the prize. Run the race, Hunter! The Lord loves you more than I ever could. He has prepared a wonderful place in heaven for you, and until that day, I pray that you will feel and know how dearly loved you are. Thank you for being such an incredible young man.

Hunter's Day of Hope for Children is tonight. It should be a lot of fun, but I have to be honest with you, Hunter: sometimes I don't want to share you with everyone else. I wish I could capture you and take you away so the two of us could be together...just you and me, without all the distractions. Wouldn't that be cool? We could do all the fun things you love to do, except bugs and reptiles and stuff like that. Maybe someday we'll do it, okay?

Heavenly Father, thank You for revealing Yourself to us through Hunter. Thank You for helping us learn, grow, and change as a result of suffering. Thank You for giving us a greater, lasting hope through Your Son. Thank You for the life and breath You give to Hunter each day. Your power is evident and magnified through his little life. Help us to persevere, no matter what.

February 17, 2005 (The Reptile Guy)—I can't believe I allowed a baby alligator to sit on your lap. I know how much you like Steve Irwin, the Crocodile Hunter, but having one in our house is crazy, don't you think? It's a good thing you and Robert are so brave, because Mommy doesn't like alligators. I still can't believe all the creatures Mr. Jeff brought to the house today. I'm so happy you and Robert were able to enjoy everything, just the two of you (and the paparazzi, of course). I know you had a blast with all the animals.

My favorite part of today was when Robert washed your hair in the Jacuzzi. I'm crying just thinking about it. He loves you so much. He really wanted to sleep over tonight, too. It broke my heart to tell him no. Maybe he can some other time, okay, buddy? What an unbelievable friendship you boys have.

March 25, 2005—Hunterboy, thank you for praying at our prayer party the other day. I would love to hear what you said to Jesus. Did you tell Him that you want a horse? Grammie is trying to convince me to buy a horse for you and your sisters. She's even talked to Aunt Chris about it. I think we'll stick with riding Bambi and watching Young Black Stallion.

Your new teacher, Ms. Bonnie, is wonderful, isn't she?

I thought Ms. Susan was great, but God continues to surprise us.

The eggs you colored today are beautiful, young man. Easter is in a couple days and I just might have to hide some of your eggs, if that's okay. I know you've been reading through the story of the resurrection. This is our hope, Hunter, the one we cling to with all that we are. Jesus is more than a Rescue Hero. He did it all so that you and I have hope beyond this life...hope beyond your suffering. There will be a day when you will finish this race, and when you do, Jesus will be there to carry you over the finish line. One day at a time, soldier.

April 7, 2005—What a great band practice the Hopesters had today [Hunter's little band, made up of our family and members of Team Hunter]. You were jamming along right to the beat with your bells, Hunter. You have always loved music, so it's fitting that you would be in a band. Justin [my cousin] loves practicing with you. I think if he could, he would teach you how to play the guitar. He would do anything for you.

Hunter is 46 inches tall now and growing, and he weighs 52.5 pounds.

May 7, 2005—Hunter, I don't know if you know this or not, but Robert has been over seven times in the last month. Wow. I really like the new tie-dye shirt he got you. We'll have to make sure you wear it the next time he comes over.

Erin's birthday party was so fun, wasn't it? She turned double-digits, ten years old. Do you like her new pet hamster, Winslow? He kind of smells, and you know Mommy's going to have to clean his cage because Erin will probably forget. Gross.

Even though your sister is busy with school and her friends, she always makes time for you. She loves you so much. Erin has asked me a few times if she could take care of you and sleep with you through the night, but I told her no. I'm sorry that I can't let her, Hunter. I know you understand.

May 26, 2005—Thank you for planting flowers with me today. You're more beautiful than all the flowers in the whole world. You lost two teeth in the last week—way to go!

July 2, 2005—Hunter, you have the best, best friend in the world. Today was "new van day" and your buddy Robert insisted on trying out your wheelchair in the van before you got in. He wanted to make sure you would be able to toler-ate your new ride. What an amazing friend.

Once we had him strapped into your Quickie wheelchair and rolled into the back of the van, you should have heard him, Hunter. He made sure we knew exactly how every single bump felt. He was very still and so serious. We told him he could relax, but he said, "This is too important for Hunter. I need to make sure it's just right for him."

That's what friends do; they encourage you and support you in good times and bad. Robert is a true best friend. He would do anything for you. Maybe you should let him beat you in UNO the next time you play. He would like that, don't you think?

I love when he holds your hand and sings "I Could Sing of Your Love Forever" to you. The friendship and love you two boys have will endure forever.

"A friend loves at all times" (Prov. 17:17).

July 15, 2005 (Ellicottville, NY—Hunter's Haven Lodge:
Hunter's Hope Family and Medical Symposium)—Daddy was
telling you all about his Alaskan bear hunt today. He loves
sharing his hunting adventures with you. He's a great story-
teller, isn't he? How about that telephone he bought not too
long ago—the one that lets out animal sounds every time it
rings? He thinks it's the greatest thing. Silly Daddy.

All the Hunter's Hope kids will be coming up to the lodge
to visit. Your friends are great. They're brave like you, Hunter.
Very brave. What a blessing to be able to help all your buddies through Hunter's Hope. It means a lot to the families.

Hunter, you've been doing so well lately. Except for the
few trips we had to make to the hospital for a tube change
and other minor things, you've been really good. In fact, when
I saw you actually doing your own leg exercises the other
day, opening and closing your legs all by yourself like a beautiful butterfly, I thought God was giving me a glimpse of your
healing. I'm serious, Hunter, that's what I thought. The more
you grow, the more of heaven I see every day. Nothing will
ever compare to watching you love life like you do. You are a
taste of heaven. You really are.

I know how much you enjoy reading Mommy's journals, so
here's a few more for you, brave one:

I Love...

...that you are so sensitive to other people's feelings.

...that you are ticklish like Mommy, especially your feet.

...that you keep me on my toes.

...that you never complain.

...who God made you to be.

...when people ask me how you are doing.

...that you are a reminder of all that is good.

...that you are a good listener.

...when you wear sunglasses and a baseball hat.

...when you take real deep breaths.

...brushing your big boy teeth.

...your name—Hunter.

...praying for you.

...kissing you.

...watching you sleep.

...running my fingers through your hair.

...talking about you.

...being your mother.

...that God is in control of your life.

...that someday you and I will be in heaven with Jesus forever.

Chapter 13

August 5, 2005

On August 4, 2005, the limo had just arrived to pick us up for the Kenny Chesney–Gretchen Wilson concert. It was five o'clock and our friends were waiting in the kitchen while Jim and I finished getting ready. Kimmy was babysitting the girls, and Hunter was at my mom and dad's house.

I wasn't in a concert mood. The kids and I had just spent the last five nights at my parents' house while attending Kingdom Bound, a huge four-day Christian music festival near Attica. After spending the last few days ride-hopping and concert-going with a bunch of kids, I was exhausted. I just wanted to stay home. I was also scheduled to tape a local television show the following morning, and I needed to prepare for it, so the girls and I had come home. Meanwhile, Hunter stayed at my parents' because it was my mom's night to take care of him.

While Jim finished getting ready upstairs, I was downstairs going over the bedtime routine with Kimmy. And then the phone rang.

"It's your mom," Kimmy said as she handed me the phone.

My mother and I talked to each other all the time, so I wasn't surprised that she was calling. Unfortunately, that conversation was the beginning of the worst twenty-four hours of my entire life.

"Hello."

"Jill, I don't think Hunter's acting like himself. I think something's wrong."

"What do you mean?"

"He's just so quiet."

"How do his lungs sound? What's his temperature?" I probed with the usual array of Hunter health questions.

"His lungs sound okay and his fever is...Jill, I just think you should come here," my mother said as she started to cry. I sensed fear and frustration in her voice. I knew in that moment something was seriously wrong.

My mother was meticulous regarding Hunter's care. And not just his physical needs, but everything that pertained to his overall health. I never worried when she took care of him. The nights she slept with him, I was able to sleep. Whenever she was in charge of the Kelly house, I could relax. "Okay, Mom, I'll come right over."

After I hung up the phone, Kimmy assured, "The girls will be fine here with me, Jill. You better go."

I felt anxious and apprehensive. Besides being worried about Hunter, all the other couples were now waiting in the limo and I was about to tell Jim he would have to go solo—again. Although we occasionally made time for each other, he was used to being without me. My life revolved around Hunter's care, and whether Jim liked it or not, so did his. Still, I knew he'd be very disappointed.

When I walked upstairs to tell Jim I wasn't going, he was fussing around the room. "Are you ready?" he asked.

He didn't look at me or he would've known something was wrong.

"Jim, I can't go," I said. "My mom just called, and something's wrong with Hunter. He's not acting like himself, and she thinks I need to come over and make sure he's okay."

"What's wrong with him? Can't your mother take care of him?" he asked with a puzzled look.

"I don't know what's wrong. That's why my mom wants me to come there."

Tears filled my eyes and anger filled my heart. *Doesn't he get it?* I thought to myself. *Nothing else matters when Hunter's sick—nothing.*

"Everybody's outside waiting to go," Jim said, frustration pushing its way into his tone. "What am I supposed to do, Jill?"

At this point I was so worked up that I lashed out at Jim and said some things I would later deeply regret: "You know what? Someday you're going to regret not spending time with Hunter. All you care about is yourself. Who cares about the stupid concert? Who cares about anything else? Hunter is sick. I'm going to my mom's."

I turned around, walked back downstairs, and kissed the girls good-bye.

The long drive to my parents' house gave me time to vent my frustrations. I was so mad at Jim. Why did everything and everybody else come before our family? There was so much I wanted to say to him, and yet I needed to keep my mouth shut for the sake of trying to trust God in the midst of our broken relationship.

When I arrived at my parents' house it was close to seven o'clock. My mom was just getting Hunter out of the swimming pool and Ellen, Hunter's nurse, was helping her get Hunter situated in his stroller.

I knelt down next to Hunter and ran my fingers through his wet, wavy hair. He was lying on his side, wrapped up in a beach towel. "Hi Hunterboy, what's going on?" I asked. "Did you have a nice swim? I came back to Grammie's to see you and to make sure you're okay. You look great, Hunter."

As I continued to run my fingers through his hair, I looked up at Ellen. "How's his temp after being in the pool?"

"We haven't checked it, but let's do that, okay, Hunter?" Ellen grabbed the thermometer and slowly tucked it under his arm.

Beep, beep, beep went the alarm. "Oh my, your temperature is perfect. It's 98.6," Ellen exclaimed as she tucked the thermometer back under the stroller.

I said with excitement, "I don't think your temp has ever been 98.6! That's so cool, Hunter. And you look and smell so good, all fresh and clean. Let's get you in the house for some chest PT, okay, buddy?"

We strolled Hunter over to the deck door and into the house. Just then my dad hollered from the kitchen, "Dinner's ready!"

I motioned to my mom and Ellen. "You go ahead and eat dinner, and I'll do Hunter's chest therapy."

"Let me help you get him over to the bed first, Jill," Ellen said. We wheeled Hunter into my parents' room, and I picked him up and started walking toward their bed when Ellen stopped me. "Well, Hunter, it looks like Mommy gets to hold you for a few minutes because your bed's not ready yet."

I made my way over to the couch and sat down with Hunter. While I held him, I marveled at how he looked and sounded. Despite the fact that he hadn't been acting like himself the past few days, he looked great. He didn't sound congested at all, which was unusual but good. By the time we got him settled in bed for therapy, it was almost nine o'clock. My mom and Ellen went to eat dinner and I started Hunter's bedtime routine.

"All that swimming in the pool made you so tired, Hunter," I said with a smile. "You relax and Mommy will give you chest PT, okay, pumpkin boy? When you're all done, Grammie's going to sleep with you and Mommy's going to go home tonight, okay?" He slowly blinked once to respond.

Depending on how Hunter was feeling and how his lungs sounded, his chest therapy usually took at least two hours. It was close to eleven by the time Hunter was done with everything.

The reason I remember the exact time everything happened is because we kept a daily schedule for Hunter, writing down everything he did and when he did it. I have a DayMinder for every year he was alive, 1997–2005. On August 4, 2005, this is what's written:

6:30 a.m. Albuterol & vest treatment - temp. 102.5 - lying on right side

8:45 a.m. Calcium & magnesium - temp. 102.9 - lying on left side

9:00 a.m. Albuterol & vest treatment - temp. 103.2 - cold compresses

10:00 a.m. Multivitamin - heart rate 158-164 - oxygen saturation 97%

11:00 a.m. Jacuzzi with Grammie - temp. 102.7

12:15 p.m. Out of Jacuzzi - temp. 98.4

12:45 p.m. Albuterol & vest treatment

3:00 p.m. Hanging out in stroller - temp. 100.3

5:00 p.m. Albuterol & vest treatment - temp. 101.3

6:30 p.m. Swimming with Grammie - having fun and very calm

7:00 p.m. Mommie's here! - out of pool - temp. 98.6

9:00 p.m. Albuterol & vest therapy - Carafate - Prilosec

10:00 p.m. Tummy & chest therapy

12:00 a.m. Tobi treatment - Cipro

2:00 a.m. Albuterol & vest therapy - temp. 103

3:00 a.m. Tummy

4:30 a.m. 911 call

By the time I was ready to head home, it was midnight and I was exhausted. Hunter was asleep on his belly, so I kissed his left cheek and whispered in his ear, "I love you, buddy, and I'll see you soon. Grammie's here with you now."

"He'll be fine, Jill. You better get home so you can get some rest before tomorrow. I'll call you in the morning," my mother reassured me.

Before leaving I hugged her and reminded her, "Make sure you call me in the morning. If he doesn't seem right to you or if he has a hard time during the night, we'll call Dr. Sharp again and see what he thinks. Okay?" Dr. Sharp was Hunter's lung doctor.

I fought the urge to turn around and go back to my parents' house the entire ride home. But I was so tired, and knew I needed to get some sleep, so I kept driving. I thought about how peaceful Hunter looked when I kissed him good-bye. He looked beautiful. And he was so tired he was snoring. I loved the sound of Hunter's breathing, especially when he snored, because I knew he was sound asleep.

Jim still wasn't home from the concert when I got back to our house. It was after one in the morning by the time I snuck in to kiss the girls good-night and sent Cassie home (another member of Team Hunter; she came to watch the girls after Kimmy left). I then washed up, went to bed in Camryn's room, and instantly fell into an exhausted sleep.

At about 4:45 a.m. I was suddenly awakened when Jim burst into the room. "Jill, your dad just called and they're rushing Hunter to the hospital."

Jim was half-awake and flustered. Jolted by the suddenness of everything, I got out of bed.

"Here, call your dad." Jim handed me the phone as I blew by him and ran down the stairs.

"Dad, what's going on? What's wrong with Hunter?" I pleaded as I held the phone with one hand and quickly changed clothes with the other.

"Jill, Hunter stopped breathing."

"What do you mean, he stopped breathing?"

Before I got to my truck I realized I was talking on our house phone, so I immediately called my father back on my cell.

"Dad, where are they taking Hunter?"

"They're taking him to Warsaw Hospital."

"No, no, they can't take him to Warsaw. They don't know him there! Dad, he has to go to Children's Hospital. They won't know how to take care of him at Warsaw," I urged.

"Jill, he might not even make it to Warsaw."

"I'm on my way."

I drove as fast as I could, but it still took me an hour to get to the hospital. I sobbed and pleaded with God the entire drive. "No, no, please God, no."

When I arrived my dad was at the bottom of the entrance road, waving with both hands to direct me where to go. I pulled into the outpatient parking area and ran into the emergency room.

Immediately I saw my mother; her face was drenched in tears. Extreme dread overcame me and I thought, *This is it. Hunter is going to die.* She quickly directed me to the first room on the left, where at least six people dressed in hospital scrubs were trying to save my son. I maneuvered my way over to Hunter's side and looked into his eyes.

He didn't acknowledge me. He didn't try to turn his head toward me. He didn't blink. He just lay there staring at the ceiling. The only movement I noticed in the room came from the nurse positioned above my son who was administering CPR.

My voice cracked as I whispered in Hunter's ear, "Hunter, Hunter, Mommy's here now. You're going to be just fine, little buddy. I'm here now. I love you, Hunter. Everything's going to be okay."

In that moment my entire essence became acutely aware that Hunter was already gone, but I prayed anyway. "God, please do something. Please. Help Hunter. Help him to breathe. Please, God. Please!"

I fell to my knees in desperation. The hospital gurney made a dull squeaking sound as the emergency room crew took turns giving Hunter CPR. Every time they stopped to see if his heart would beat again on its own, the line was flat. But they kept trying.

In Jim's Own Words

I don't remember if someone told me to go to Children's Hospital instead of Warsaw Hospital, or if I just assumed it because Jill told her dad that Hunter should go to Children's, but unfortunately that's where I went.

The emergency room was busy when I got to Children's, so I waited about fifteen minutes, which seemed like an hour. Finally I went up to the desk to find out what was going on. I asked the nurse if she knew when Hunter would be arriving. She just looked at me like she had no idea what I was talking about: "Mr. Kelly, let me check on that for you." She got up and walked over to another nurse and then came back and said, "We have no information on Hunter right now, Mr. Kelly. Are you sure he's coming here?"

At that point I started to get really upset. I explained to her that initially they were going to take Hunter to Warsaw

Hospital but . . . As soon as I said, "Warsaw Hospital," she interrupted, "Hold on a minute, Mr. Kelly. Let me see if I can find out what's going on."

She got up from her desk, out of my sight. Within seconds she came whipping around the corner and said, "Hunter's at Warsaw Hospital. You need to go there right away." I could tell something was wrong by the way she was acting.

As I ran out to my truck, I realized I had no idea where Warsaw Hospital was. I got directions from someone as fast as I could. I was so mad that I had wasted all that time at Children's when Hunter was at Warsaw.

Once I got out of the city of Buffalo, I ended up behind a car that was moving along pretty fast. But then a cop went by and I saw him turn around in my rearview mirror. I thought to myself, he better not pull me over—the guy in front of me is going faster than I am. When I heard the siren and saw the flashing lights, I automatically slowed down, still thinking the cop would pass me and pull the car in front of me over. But he didn't. He pulled me over.

When he got up to the car, I was about to explain what was going on when he said, "Oh thank God it's you, Mr. Kelly. We got a call about your son and I've been looking for your vehicle. Please follow me. I'm going to escort you to Warsaw Hospital."

He ran back to his police car and I followed him to the hospital. At that point I was scared. However, I knew Hunter was tough, and he had always pulled through before. So I thought for sure he would pull through again.

I'd watched Hunter struggle so many times and battle back. He was resilient. I thought about the many times he had been in the ICU on a respirator with pneumonia and the times we were sure it was the end of the road. I just couldn't let myself think he would die.

When I pulled into the emergency lot to park the car, a man stopped me. Before I could say anything he said, "We'll park your car for you, Mr. Kelly."

"That's okay, I'll park it," I replied.

However, he insisted and said once again, "You just go on in, Mr. Kelly. We'll take care of your car."

I thought that was strange, but I realized why when I got inside the first set of doors to the emergency room.

Time seemed to stand still. My mother came over to where I was kneeling on the floor next to Hunter. "He needs to go to Children's Hospital, Mom—right now," I pleaded. "They know what to do to help him. He has to go there."

I begged my mother to do something, anything, to make things better. "What about his lungs? Maybe he needs to be on a respirator."

"Jill, he's already on a respirator." My mother gently tried to explain that the hospital crew was doing everything possible to save Hunter and that a team from Children's was on their way.

The frenzied activity of the hospital staff continued. I could hear the sound of the machines surrounding my son. Tubes were coming from everywhere on his pale little body. Every effort was being made to save Hunter's life.

Suddenly I felt very light-headed and queasy. I looked down at Hunter and then turned to my mom: "I don't feel so good." I was quickly whisked away into an adjacent room and laid down on a gurney. I thought I was going to pass out; I was sure I'd throw up.

My mother started to gently rub my back. Anxious to return to Hunter's side, I sat back up. Just then a nurse walked in and handed my mother a can of orange juice and said, "She should drink this." I quickly downed a few sips of orange juice and got up from the gurney.

As my mother and I rushed back to Hunter's room, a doctor came up and said to me, "Mrs. Kelly, would you like to take a look at Hunter's chest x-ray?" I followed him while my mom returned to Hunter.

He led me to where Hunter's x-ray was displayed. Much to my shock, his lungs looked great. Better than ever. I had looked at every one of Hunter's chest x-rays through the years, and inexplicably, this time he didn't have pneumonia.

It wasn't his lungs this time, so what was it?

Is it his heart?

There has to be something we can do, I thought to myself.

As my eyes filled with tears, I turned to the doctor. "Is there any other machine Hunter can go on?"

The doctor's response is forever etched in my memory: he shook his head and said, "We love Hunter, too. We've done everything we possibly could, Mrs. Kelly."

I'll never forget that moment. Standing there in an unfamiliar hospital with a doctor I did not know, with complete strangers still struggling to draw any signs of life out of my only son, a sense of gratitude and peace quieted my soul. And for just a second, I was okay.

Because they loved Hunter, too.

I hurried back to Hunter's side just as two nurses from Children's Hospital arrived. They had flown by helicopter and had gotten there as fast as they could. (I would find out later that they knew before they came there was nothing more they could do for Hunter. But they came anyway.) I immediately recognized one of them and felt relieved and hopeful again. She came over to where I was sitting and kneeled down beside me. I looked at her and asked in desperation, "Is there anything more you can do?"

She shook her head and quietly said, "I'm so sorry, Jill. I'm so sorry."

My mother came over, wrapped her arms around me—and we fell apart. Side by side we sat there next to our beloved little boy, just weeping, sharing our anguish, while the medical team continued to work on Hunter. After what seemed like hours, I looked up at the nurse closest to me and reluctantly said, "Please stop."

And she did.

They all did.

And it was silent.

No one said a word. The room was quiet.

The realization of what had just happened shattered me in unimaginable and indescribable ways.

As I sat in the silence, with my head lying next to Hunter's body, Jim burst through the door. He rushed to Hunter's side and began to talk to him. "Hunter, Daddy is here now, little buddy. I'm here." Jim's eyes filled with tears as he took one deep breath and then another. I couldn't bear to watch Jim touch our son's lifeless body, so I left the room.

I don't remember what happened after I left Jim alone with Hunter, but I do recall that I felt completely alone and hopeless. Hunter was gone. How I made it out of the emergency room that morning, I'll never know.

———

As Jim and I drove home together, I became acutely aware that life all around me continued to go on. *How is that possible?* I thought. *My son is dead. Life will never be the same without Hunter.*

My mother sat in the backseat in silence. I had asked her to ride with us so that she could be there when we told the girls about their brother. When we were almost home, my mother broke the silence and said with tears, "Oh my goodness, today is Robert's birthday."

I turned around and just looked at her. I was speechless.

I can't believe Hunter went to heaven on his best friend's birthday.

I can't believe this is happening.

I was in shock.

I couldn't think.

I couldn't talk.

I wanted to scream.

I wanted to disappear.

Sorrow.

Grief.

August 6, 2005—My heart is shattered. How can I live without you, buddy? I long to be near you. Oh Lord, the pain is more than I can bear. Please take me, too.

Jim was a warrior on the football field. © Jim Bush. Special thanks to Jim Bush for permission to publish this photo.

November 2, 1995— Jim proposed and I said yes. © Daniel Palumbo

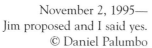

May 18, 1996— Everything about our wedding day was perfect. © Daniel Palumbo

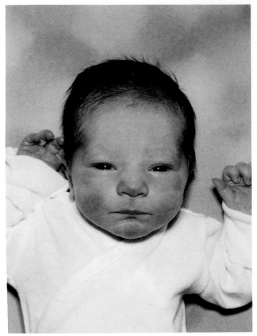

Hunter's picture taken just hours after he was born, February 14, 1997.

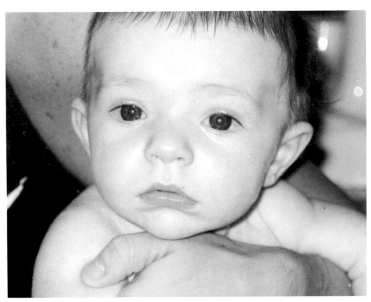

June 24, 1997: This photo was taken the day Hunter was diagnosed with Krabbe Leukodystrophy. He was four months old.

Taking a quick nap.

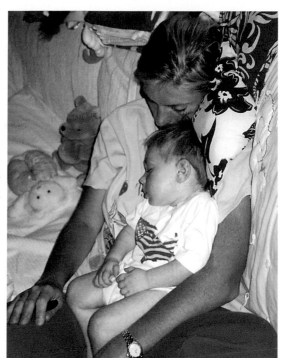

Bambi was Hunter's favorite horse, so we tried to visit her as often as we could. Of course Camryn had to ride, too.

I'll never forget the day we took Hunter sledding. He loved it. After we were done we sat in the snow and talked about how much fun we had.

Hunter making pottery.

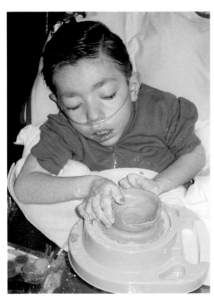

Hunter trying out his therapy vest for the very first time. I was so nervous for him.

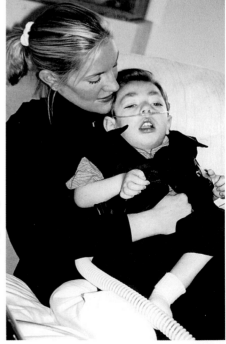

Hunter with a real
chameleon on his head.

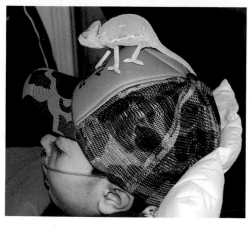

In his stander, Hunter
felt big and tall.

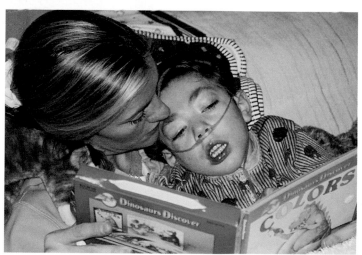

I loved reading to Hunter.

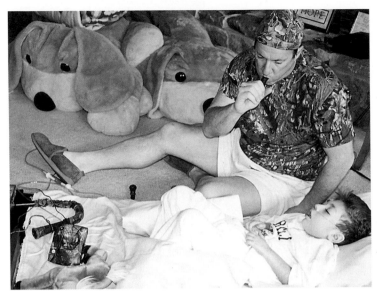

Jim loves to hunt. Here he's showing Hunter his entire collection of animal calls: elk, turkey, and deer.

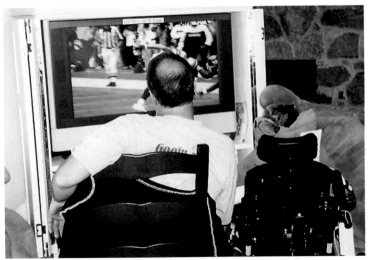

Jim loved to share his passion for football with Hunter. This is one of my favorite pictures because it shows the two boys hanging out together doing what most boys like to do...watch football.

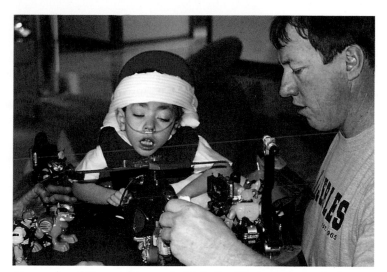

Hunter loved Rescue Heroes. I think Jim liked playing with them as much as Hunter did.

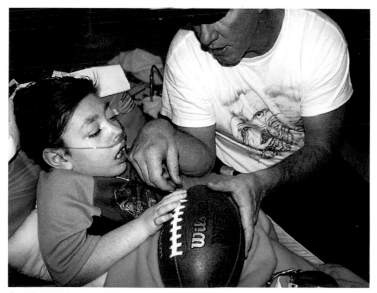

Daddy teaching HB how to grip a football.

This is one of my favorite photos of the three kids, taken during our 2003 Christmas card photo session.
© Brody Wheeler

Camryn helping Hunter stir pumpkin pie mix. I love the way she's looking at her brother.

We caught Cam red-handed trying to give Hunter chest therapy. . . . What a stinker!

Hunter and Robert are having a blast squirting Camryn with loads of Silly String! Elizabeth had just as much fun as the kids.

Dancing together.

Just hanging out.

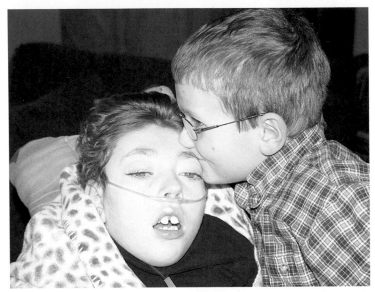

Hunter and Robert had an extraordinary friendship. They had so much fun together.

Robert, testing Hunter's wheelchair.

Hunter looked forward to his adventures at his grandparents' home in Attica, especially his visits to see Bambi.

My dad hugging Hunter.

I still can't believe we took Hunter snowmobiling. I'm driving and my mother is holding Hunter. We had a blast.

This is my favorite picture of my mother and Hunter.

My cousin Justin is a gifted musician who spent a lot of time with Hunter. Here they're having band practice for the Hopesters.

Baking a chocolate chip cake with Marion and Elizabeth.

Hunter was holding the fishing pole before this picture was taken. My aunt Dodie is showing Hunter his big catch.

Kristin and Hunter playing with shaving foam.

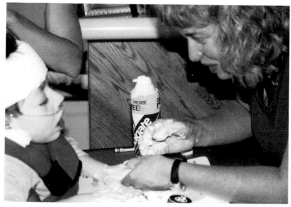

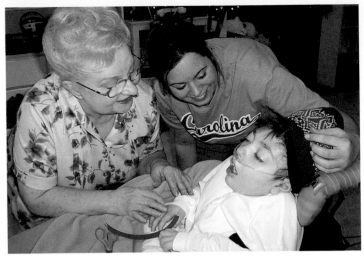

Reggie and Jennifer talking to Hunterboy.

Ms. Bonnie, Hunterboy's teacher, making a fun apple art project.

The kids and me before we all walked out onto the Buffalo Bills' field with Jim for the Wall of Fame ceremony, 2002.

We celebrate life through our Every Steps Walk held at various times throughout the year across the United States.

Before the start of the walk, we write messages on balloons to our kids in heaven and then release them.

On September 19, 2008, in a simple yet beautiful ceremony, Jim and I renewed our wedding vows. © www.pchoatephoto.com

This family photo was taken at the 2009 Hunter's Hope Candlelight Ball, a black-tie event we hold every year in Buffalo, New York. © Brody Wheeler

Chapter 14

Memories Everywhere

August 9, 2005—I don't know if there are any tears left to cry. It was beautiful today. Not a cloud in the sky. A perfect day to bury my son.

I hate this. I want to run, but there's nowhere to hide. HELP!

It must have been horrible for Robert to walk in front of the casket that carried the lifeless body of his best friend. He's too young for all this heartbreak and pain. I wanted to hug him and never let go. I'm going to miss Robert.

I don't remember much of what Pastor Greg said at Hunter's Celebration of Eternal Life service, but I do remember our nanny, Jill Kivett, singing "His Eye Is on the Sparrow." That had to be so hard. She used to sing that to Hunter all the time. I'm so thankful she could be here today.

It was hard to concentrate and take it all in when Camryn kept sobbing in my arms. She just kept crying and crying and there was nothing I could do to help her. So I just held her. I need You to hold me, Father. I can't believe he's gone. What am I going to do? Help me to remember

*everything about him. Help me to remember everything You
taught us.*

*Hunter was an amazing little boy. I'm drowning in tears.
But I know that You are close to the brokenhearted and
save those who are crushed in spirit....*

I was in shock. In a whirlwind of just a few days, I had said
good-bye to my son. On a beautiful sunny summer day I sat in the
front pew at our church—completely numb during his Celebration of Eternal Life service—placed a white rose and small marble
cross on my son's casket...and then everything was over.

It was all over.

Everyone went home. Food started to spoil in our refrigerator.
The girls wanted to go to the movies. And Jim went out of town
for an appearance. But my heart was shattered and lifeless.

Memories of Hunter's life were everywhere. His medications
were in the refrigerator and all over the kitchen counter to the
right of the sink. His suction machines, towels, dirty sheets, and
pillowcases were still in the laundry room. His books, his toys,
his movies and artwork were scattered around the playroom....
He was everywhere. He had gotten a hundred on his last book
report and math test, and both were still proudly displayed on our
kitchen cupboard. His clothes were in my closet and neatly folded
in my drawers because we shared a room.

My bedroom had become Hunter's bedroom. Because of the
advanced care he needed throughout the night, we ended up
sleeping in the same bed. He was always on my left.

When I woke up the morning after Hunter died, the first
thought that ran through my mind was, *He's not here. He'll never
snuggle with me again.*

What was I supposed to do with all of Hunter's clothes? Box
everything up and put them in storage? Should I give some of

them to my nephews Ben and Zac? Zac was only eleven days older than Hunter, so Hunter's clothes would probably have fit him. But that would be so hard. His shirts especially held precious memories. As I mentioned in the journals, the last year of Hunter's life he lost his involuntary blink, so we had to put special gel in his eyes every hour to keep his eyes moist. Inevitably the gel would get all over Hunter's shirts, and it wouldn't come out in the wash. I just couldn't imagine giving his little gel-stained shirts away.

What about all his Rescue Heroes? He had every one of the action figures and all the vehicles and accessories that went along with them.

I didn't want the two huge oxygen tanks to leave either. We'd had oxygen tanks in the house before Hunter was even born; they were familiar to us. Jim's mother, Alice, had been on oxygen because of her emphysema. When she died, the tanks left. And then a year and a half later, Hunter was diagnosed with Krabbe disease and the tanks came back. I missed the sound of the air bubbling through the water attached to the tank.

What am I supposed to do with Hunter's Quickie wheelchair? And should we sell Hunter's van made special for him? The van Hunter and Robert cruised around in the first day Hunter ever rode in it? The van we only had for two months before Hunter died?

What about his therapy vest? Unique memories were literally plastered all over it in an array of colorful stickers filled with meaning. Before we would put any stickers on Hunter's vest, we'd always show them to him first to get his approval. He would blink once for "yes" to let us know if he liked the sticker. If he didn't blink, it didn't go on. There were three Spider-Man stickers on the vest along with four glittery frog stickers. A big sticker of Davey and Goliath was on the front of the machine. Hunter loved Davey and Goliath. My aunt Dodie, one of Hunter's nurses, searched everywhere for videos and other Davey and Goliath paraphernalia. Hunter even had a lunch box with the dynamic duo on it.

"U.S. Army" and "God Bless America" stickers were on the vest machine, too. My mother gave Hunter the nickname "Soldier Boy" because he was so incredibly courageous and brave. As I looked at those stickers, two memories came vividly to mind. First, I could hear my mother singing "Soldier Boy" to Hunter in the Jacuzzi. She was always singing to Hunter, and he loved her voice. I knew I'd miss hearing my mother sing.

Then I remembered Hunter's 2003 Good Scout Award for Bravery, given to him by the Boy Scouts of America–Greater Niagara Frontier Council. Many of our family and friends had attended the awards ceremony. Robert was there to celebrate and support his best friend, too. Having the boys together, decked out in their best attire, was a sight to see. Hunter was feeling good and he looked so handsome.

Before the ceremony I talked to Hunter about the normal protocol when someone receives an award of such magnitude. I explained how important it was for him and our entire family to acknowledge how grateful we were for his honor. We talked about what it means to be truly brave and courageous, and I told him how incredibly brave I thought he was.

Together we wrote an acceptance speech for Hunter's award. As I discussed with him what he might possibly say to the audience, he'd blink in agreement at the suggestions he liked, and I'd write the words down. I only wanted Hunter's words to be heard, not mine.

Here's what Hunter said in his acceptance speech after receiving the Good Scout Award for Bravery:

First of all, I just have to tell you that I'm feeling pretty important with this fancy shirt and tie on. I only dress up like this once a year for our family Christmas picture, so this is so cool for me.

This is such a great day! Thank you so much for honoring me this afternoon with the Boy Scout Award for Bravery. I did not know what it meant to be brave until now. For a six-year-old boy to stand up here in front of all of you—now that's brave.

When my mom and I talked about bravery the other day, a few thoughts came to my mind. To me, bravery is:

Like a tiny fish in a big blue sea or a birdie learning to fly
Being strong even when it hurts
Telling you how I feel deep in my heart
Watching kids run and play and telling them, "Great job"
Stretching my arms and moving my head all by myself
Catching my breath

I'm very happy to be Hunter James Kelly. Although I am unable to do a lot of things, I am able to do what is most important—and that is to love. God is so good to me. He blessed me with a very important mission here on earth, and all of you are helping me to achieve it. Hunter's Hope is so special to my family and me. You all have been so generous in helping us to raise awareness and funds to help my friends with this terrible disease. And believe me, this disease is awful.

But more important than all of that, God asked me to teach all of you about Him and His amazing love for all of us. Sometimes we get carried away with the things of this world that really don't matter, when all that really matters is that we fulfill the purpose for which God created each one of us. My purpose is to show all of you that God's love is the best, and that prayer really can move mountains and give strength to the weak and hope to those who have none.

You see, it's not about me; it's all about Him. I love being a six-year-old boy, but I love being God's little warrior even more. I'm thankful for God and all the people that love me and help me to be brave. Please keep me in your prayers, and thank you again for this very special honor.

There wasn't a dry eye in the room that day. What a precious memory. A memory birthed from a sticker on a therapy vest.

I was surrounded by such reminders. But regardless of how wonderful a memory might be, each one also had the power to immobilize me. *Should I give away some of the sources of those memories to avoid the emotional pain?* It was just so hard to make decisions about anything. I felt paralyzed.

Laundry could wait.

The dishes could wait.

Quiet time could wait.

My life could wait.

Chapter 15

Unexpected Grace

The day after Hunter's funeral I dusted off a copy of Randy Alcorn's *Heaven*—a book I had barely started reading months before Hunter died. I had to get out of the house, away from what life was starting to become without Hunter, so I threw my book in a backpack and headed to my mom and dad's house. Erin and Camryn were busy playing with friends, and that made it easier for me to leave them at home with Jim.

In my grief, I needed to be near where my boy was during the last moments of his life. I needed to touch the soft sheets he'd last slept in while they were still exactly as he'd left them. The young life that had captivated and consumed my every minute and my every thought was gone. I didn't know what to do with myself.

As I traveled the same route I always did to my parents' home, the same route that led to the hospital where Hunter had died, I tried desperately to make sense out of what had happened. So many questions were invading my mind. I wanted to know why God had allowed Hunter to take his last breath in my mother's arms instead of mine. Was He mad at me? Did He forget that I had prayed many times to be the one? If I had been there at my parents' house that morning, would Hunter still be alive?

I cried and tried to take in the beauty of the day as I drove. The sky was very blue, with a few puffy clouds scattered here and there. The sun was bright yet it wasn't hot. There was a nice cool breeze, too. It was a perfect day; just like the day Hunter took his last breath.

When I arrived in Attica I stopped by the cemetery before going on to my parents' house. The plot of land where Hunter's body was buried is right next to a war monument for fallen soldiers. *How fitting,* I thought, *that our brave little soldier was buried next to a memorial for those who have given their lives for our country.* A pile of fresh dirt was still there, waiting for grass to grow. Standing there I thought, *While I'm waiting to see Hunter again, what's he experiencing in heaven? What's heaven really like? Does Hunter have a new body right now? What's he doing? Can he see what's going on down here?* I had so many questions.

A little later, when I got to the top of my parents' driveway, my mother was standing there to greet me. I was happy to see her. "Did you stop at the cemetery?" she asked.

I responded yes and just looked at her. It was obvious that I had been crying. As we hugged, she whispered in my ear, "We'll take care of Hunter's spot, Jill. It will eventually look better than it does right now."

"I know, Mom. I know," I responded with a heavy sigh.

I walked over to a lounge chair by the pool and my mom went inside to prepare some lunch. After I got situated, I opened *Heaven* to where I had left off months before: page fifty-five— "Does 'paradise' suggest a physical place?" The more I read, the more excited and encouraged I became.

A fundamental article of the Christian faith is that the resurrected Christ now dwells in heaven. We are told that his resurrected body on Earth was physical, and that this same, physical Jesus ascended to Heaven, from which he will one day return to Earth (Acts 1:11). It seems indisputable, then, to say that there is at least one physical body in the present Heaven. If Christ's body in the intermediate Heaven has physical properties, it would stand to reason that others in Heaven might have physical forms as well, even if only temporary ones.[1]

My heart started to race as I thought to myself, *Maybe Hunter does have a physical body right now. What if God's actually revealing what my heart longs to understand?*

The more I read, the more convinced I was that God was speaking to the questions on my mourning heart.

Hebrews 12:1 tells us to "run with perseverance the race marked out for us," creating the mental picture of the Greek competitions, which were watched intently by throngs of engrossed fans sitting high up in the ancient stadiums. The "great cloud of witnesses" refers to the saints who've gone before us, whose accomplishments on the playing field of life are now part of our rich history. The imagery seems to suggest that those saints, the spiritual "athletes" of old, are now watching us and cheering us on from the great stadium of Heaven that looks down on the field of Earth. (The witnesses are said to "surround" us, not merely to have preceded us.)[2]

Picturing Hunter as an athlete watching us from the great stadium of heaven was uplifting and exciting. I thought of Jim and the thousands of fans that had cheered him on for years, and now our son was cheering us on. While we continue to press on here in the game of life, our little athlete is suited up in heaven's finest, watching and waiting. As the sun continued to warm my face that gorgeous afternoon, I thought about Hunter wearing a number 12 jersey and playing football now for the winning team—the only team that matters.

I laid my copy of *Heaven* down on my lap, closed my eyes, and started to pray: "Lord, can Hunter see us right now? Is he watching and cheering us on as we struggle to live without him? My heart overflows with questions. But knowing You is more important than having answers. Lord, help me to love You more than I miss Hunter. Thank You for—"

"Jill, lunch is ready," my mother called. I got up from my chair and headed over to help her. Then she stopped abruptly, looked up to the sky, and exclaimed, "Turn around, Jill. You're not going to believe this." When I turned and looked up, there, in the middle of the beautiful blue sky, was the letter *H* in the clouds.

"I've got to get my camera," my mother said as she handed me the lunch tray and ran back into the house.

I stared at the sky, speechless. *An H for Hunter, an H for heaven*, I said to myself as I walked over to the nearest table and set the food down. Eating could wait.

As my mother snapped a bunch of pictures, my gaze was fixed heavenward.

"Look through here," she said, handing me her camera. Though it was still there, right before my eyes, I couldn't believe what I was seeing.

Maybe we were hallucinating. Or maybe a few planes had flown by and stretched the clouds out to form a perfect *H* in the sky.

Or maybe—just maybe—the hand of a loving and compassionate God reached down into our grief that afternoon.

I didn't know, and honestly, I didn't have the energy to try to figure it all out. But what I was certain of is this: we saw a huge white *H* in the sky that day, and I'll never forget it.

After the *H*-shaped cloud started to disappear, our momentary excitement ended and feelings of sorrow returned.

"Mom, what happened?" I asked. I needed to hear the story repeatedly the first few months after Hunter's passing. I wasn't there, but she was. I wasn't in the back of the ambulance, holding Hunter's hand. Agonizing as it was, I had tried to picture everything in my mind, hoping to make sense of it all. Thankfully, as hard as it was for my mother, she was always willing to recount what had happened during those horrible moments at her house.

She was lying next to him when he stopped breathing, she said. She watched the emergency technicians try to resuscitate my son. She was with him in the ambulance as they kept trying to revive Hunter. She was there as they wheeled him into the emergency room for the last time....

My mother and I had so much to talk about, so many memories to share, and yet the emptiness and sorrow we felt were unbearable.

Later that night, while I lay restlessly in Hunter's bed trying to sleep, I remembered my book. Throwing aside the covers, I went to the closet in search of my backpack, where I found *Heaven*. I started reading where I had left off that afternoon:

Meanwhile, we on this dying Earth can relax and rejoice for our loved ones who are in the presence of Christ. As the apostle Paul tells us, though we naturally grieve at losing loved ones, we are not "to grieve like the rest of men, who have no hope" (1 Thessalonians 4:13). Our parting is not the end of our relationship, only an interruption. We have not "lost" them, because we know where they are.

They are experiencing the joy of Christ's presence in a place so wonderful that Christ called it Paradise. And one day, we're told, in a magnificent reunion, they and we "will be with the Lord forever. Therefore encourage each other with these words" (1 Thessalonians 4:17-18).[3]

A sense of peace and purpose swept over me as I closed the book and laid it on my nightstand. I was overwhelmed with gratitude to God for the encouragement the words had given me. It was a little bit of unexpected grace. At that defining moment, I determined in my heart not "to grieve like the rest of men, who have no hope" (1 Thessalonians 4:13).

Two months later, on October 5, I was surprised by another small touch of grace. I was standing in the kitchen, peering through the sliding glass doors, when I heard a thump. There, lying motionless on our back deck, was a little bird. The poor thing must have flown into the window and injured itself because it was barely breathing. I wasn't sure what to do, but I had to do something.

I scanned the kitchen for some tissues and slowly opened the door. The frail, fallen creature struggled vainly to move but couldn't. Instead, it lay there in silent fear. Gently, I nudged the helpless little thing onto the tissues and into my hands. Then, walking slowly over to the patio couch, I sat down, not fully understanding why I was so moved.

The bird was beautiful. I guessed it was a male because its bright, multihued body was striking. Stroking his soft, ruffled feathers from the top of his head to the tip of his tail seemed to soothe him, and he relaxed a bit. It was the least I could do, because it looked as if he was dying. And as I sat there cradling him, I thought about an experience I'd had just two days before Hunter died—a very similar encounter but with a different bird.

My daughters and I had been staying at my parents' house for a few days. Our breakfast was interrupted one morning by a loud noise that caused us all to jump in alarm. A disoriented bird had flown into the kitchen window. Unfortunately, before we could get to it, Max and Jake—my dad's black Labs—were trying to mess with the wounded bird. Somehow we were able to wrestle it from the snarling dogs amid the cries of Erin and Camryn, who sobbed as I cuddled the poor thing in my hands. Hunter was in his stroller not too far from all the commotion.

Although it was obvious the bird was dying, it was so beautiful, and this was such an uncommon occurrence, that I wanted Hunter to see the little creature. I walked carefully over to his stroller and knelt down next to him. Everyone crowded around and watched intently as I picked up Hunter's hand so he could pet the bird.

"Isn't he beautiful, Hunter?" I said as I moved his hand up and down across the bird's feathers. He blinked his eyes once to say yes. "Do you see how lovely this bird is? Even though he's dying, all his colors and markings are still so beautiful. The life of every creature and the breath of all mankind are in God's hand," I said. "He knew today would be the day this little creature would take its last breath. He knows everything. And even though we don't understand why things happen the way they do, God knows."

My inquisitive daughter, Camryn, interrupted me with a stream of questions: "Is he going to die, Mama? Are we going to bury him? Where are we going to put him? What are we going to do, Mama?"

"Well, Cam, we're going to find a resting place for this bird."

We found a spot near the edge of the woods and laid the little bird there.

"Can we come back and check on him?" Camryn asked earnestly.

"Sure, honey, we'll come back in a little while. Let him rest for now."

As we walked away, I knew it wouldn't be long before the bird would be gone. Of course, I didn't know it then, but it wouldn't be long before Hunter would be gone, too.

But God knew.

Now, here I was, sitting on my patio couch two months later, remembering that day in my parents' backyard and recalling what I had said to Hunter and his sisters about the death of another little bird. I suddenly realized that God had used that earlier experience to somehow prepare all of us for Hunter's death.

I wept.

And I prayed for the broken bird in my hands. "Please help this bird. He's struggling, unable to fly. Is he going to die?" And that is when I experienced a touch of God's grace, the kind of grace that would help to shepherd me through the grieving process, no matter how long it might take.

When Hunter was alive, I had hoped and prayed that he would take his last breath in my arms. The fear of losing him, or not being there for him, had consumed me for years. He was my boy, my only son. I wanted to be the one with him when he took his last breath here and his first breath in heaven. But I wasn't. And I was devastated.

My entire life had revolved around Hunter. Every breath he took was a gift. I didn't want to miss a thing. No matter where I was or who I was with, my heart and mind were with Hunter.

As time went by, we all seemed to forget that he was dying from a horrendous illness. In fact, my mother and I had actually discussed getting some more blood work done, just to confirm the diagnosis. Hunter was beating the odds. He was *living*.

So at that moment, taking care of that frail, helpless little bird took on new meaning. As the creature struggled for every breath,

I thought of Hunter and the sound of his breathing. Hunter didn't have a normal breathing pattern. When Hunter's lungs were clear, his breathing was big and full. But often, because of his inability to swallow, he would gurgle a lot with every breath. His gurgled breathing was like sweet music to my ears, especially during the night. My head was usually about a foot away from Hunter's. I slept as close to him as I possibly could so that I could hear every breath.

The tears streamed down my cheeks as I remembered these things and tried to comfort the beautiful little bird in my hands. He was still alive, but his breathing had grown very shallow. I continued to gently stroke his feathers; they were so soft and vibrant. Like Hunter's skin.

His skin was amazing; so soft and white, like a newborn baby's. It was so unique that after we laid him to rest, the funeral director—a family friend I used to babysit for—commented, "Hunter had the most beautiful skin I have ever seen." I recalled Hunter's little brown mole on his right hip and the tiny scar on his belly from where his feeding tube had been inserted. Other than that, his entire body was unblemished.

And then I remembered his hands. Even his hands were special. One of the disease markers for most Krabbe children is the clenched fist. But Hunter's hands weren't like that at all. We massaged his hands constantly, elongating his chunky fingers. To keep him from drawing his fingers into a clenched fist, we made sure he was always holding a soft stuffed animal or blanket.

I always wanted his hand in mine. My memory at that moment was so vivid that I could almost feel his strong grip. After a long night of hand-holding, he usually wouldn't let go in the morning. Whenever I would say good-bye and try to walk away, he'd squeeze my fingers. He didn't want me to leave. I never wanted to leave him either.

And I didn't want the little bird I was holding to leave. But it did, and the profoundness of the moment wrapped itself around me. Although I was not with Hunter when he took his last breath, God was. Somehow, the privilege of holding that helpless bird while he took his last breath, and the precious memories the experience provided, began to mend my broken heart. It was a moment of grace I knew I would never forget.

Chapter 16

"My Heart Doesn't Look the Same Anymore"

My heart doesn't look the same anymore, Mommy." My ten-year-old daughter, Erin, tilted her head and started to draw a broken heart with her fingers in the air. "It looks like this, and it has a big hole in it. Because Hunter's not here, I have a huge hole in my heart that can't be filled."

A fresh wave of grief swept over me as I grabbed my daughter and hugged her. I had been praying that God would show me how to help my daughters in their grieving. They dearly loved their brother. I could only guess what their little minds and hearts were thinking and feeling. I laid my head on Erin's, and we both started to cry.

"I'm nothing without Hunter, Mommy." She spoke exactly what I felt. "I am who I am because of him. I know Jesus because of Hunter."

"Someday your heart will be full again, Erin, someday...."

I felt so inadequate. What could I say or do to comfort my daughters when I needed to be comforted? We all needed comfort. The mother in me wanted to take away their pain. Yet I knew they had to experience loss and walk through grief, too. They needed to learn what only a broken heart could teach, but it was so hard watching them, even knowing that somehow it was for their good.

In the days following Hunter's death, Erin was quiet. She didn't talk about Hunter very often. In this way she was responding a lot like her dad. Camryn, on the other hand, was very emotional and outspoken. She wore her heart on her sleeve, just as I did.

At bedtime, a little over a month after Hunter died, Camryn asked me, "Mommy, will Hunter recognize us when we get to heaven? How old will Hunter be?" Before I could answer, I was bombarded with more questions.

"When I see Hunter in heaven, will he look like this?" She was holding a framed picture of her hugging Hunter. He had on a baseball hat and was looking right into the camera. It was such a great shot. I remembered when that picture was taken. It was Erin Marie's birthday party that day, and we'd had a blast.

As we continued our discussion, Camryn boldly exclaimed, "Mommy, I want Hunter to have oxygen in heaven. And I don't want him to walk there."

Erin added, "I liked his oxygen, Mommy. It wasn't a bad thing, and Hunter always looked so cute."

I tried to explain what I understood to be true about heaven. A biblical discourse wasn't needed, but a heart-to-heart was. Cam and Erin were just missing their brother.

"Hunter won't need oxygen in heaven. The only reason—"

Camryn anxiously interrupted, with attitude. "But if he doesn't have oxygen, he won't be Hunter. I won't recognize him."

I could tell that no matter what I said, it probably wouldn't make a difference to Cam, but I continued anyway. "In heaven,

Hunter doesn't need oxygen. There's no disease or sickness there. He's finally free, Cam. Free to do all the things he never could here. Isn't that so cool? I wonder what Hunter's voice sounds like. And what—"

"How did Hunter get sick, Mama?" she interrupted again.

Oh boy, I thought to myself—*here we go*. I took a deep breath and tried to explain what I didn't fully understand myself. "Well, honey, Hunter was born without a special enzyme that we all need in our brain. Because he didn't have that enzyme, his brain didn't work the way it's supposed to. We need our brain to work so that we can run and talk and eat and laugh and do all of the things we do every day."

I paused for a moment as she pondered.

"Why didn't we just give Hunter what he needed?" she asked.

How I wished it had been that easy.

"Camryn, we did everything we possibly could for your brother."

I then tried my best to satisfy Cam's childlike desire to make sense of her brother's life and death.

Finally she said, "I miss Hunter. And I'm tired. Can we pray and go to bed now?"

I pulled the covers up close to her little face and kissed her forehead. After both girls were snuggled in, I knelt beside their bed and prayed.

While I had been talking with Camryn, I wondered what Erin was thinking. She spoke up a few times during our conversation, but for the most part she just listened. I would discover a couple of weeks later how her young mind was processing everything, when we agreed to share our story with *People* magazine. If I had known the outcome of the article before the interview, I would've never agreed to do it.

In the past, whenever Jim and I shared our personal family

struggles with the media, we always had one goal in mind—to encourage families and draw awareness to Hunter's Hope. In this interview, I didn't want to talk about losing Hunter because I hadn't even processed it all yet. Instead, I wanted to talk about his life and the undeniable, indescribable joy our family experienced as a result of it. Yet as much as we tried to accentuate the incredible impact of Hunter's life, unfortunately the writer focused on the details of his death.

All three of our children had participated in and listened to numerous interviews we'd done throughout the years, but Erin was unusually upset after our *People* interview. As I hugged her tightly and tried to console her, I thought about what we might have said that would've caused her to cry. As much as I could recall, I was fairly confident that Jim and I hadn't said anything she didn't already know.

We'd always been very careful about what we said in front of the kids. Although maybe a tad extreme, we made every effort to keep negative talk far from their innocent, impressionable ears. Life was hard enough, so we tried to protect them as much as possible.

While Jim and I said good-bye to the magazine crew, my mother comforted Erin. As soon as they were gone, I motioned for Erin to come and sit next to me on the couch. Her face was blotchy from crying, and she appeared exhausted. "Honey, please talk to me," I urged as I brushed her bangs away from her face so I could see her blue eyes.

"Mommy, how come I'm not a carrier like you and Daddy and Camryn? I want to be a carrier of the gene, too."

I was stunned and didn't know what to say. Before I could respond, tears filled my eyes.

Erin continued, "I wanted to have a baby someday just like Hunter. What if I wanted to have a Krabbe baby?"

Her words broke my heart. I knew she loved Hunter, but I had no idea how much she had identified with him and his illness.

———

During the four years following Hunter's death, Camryn and Erin have been doing well, emotionally and spiritually. Yet they were different ages when Hunter died, and they have distinct personalities. They have kept the memories of Hunter alive in wonderfully unique ways.

While I was writing this chapter, my freckle-faced daughter Camryn insisted on interrupting me. The signs she made and posted on both doors of the office read: *"Keep Out Of The Office While She Is Writing. Thanks, ☺."* But even with the doors closed and my hands typing away on the keyboard, she couldn't seem to stay away or follow her own instructions.

"Mommy, you have to come outside right now. There's something really special I want you to see."

"Camryn, I'm writing. What is it, honey? Can it wait until I'm done?" I responded with a big sigh as I turned and looked at her.

"I can't tell you. It's very special. Come on, Mom. Please come outside and I'll show you."

Reluctantly, I got up from my desk, slipped my sneakers on, and walked outside with Cam.

It was a gorgeous summer day. After I walked outside, I was thankful Camryn decided to interrupt me. I needed a break. Writing this memoir had been a heartrending journey, far more difficult than I would've ever imagined. On that day I had struggled more than usual. But the blessings of God continue to amaze and encourage me.

"Just follow me, Mommy."

Camryn's mouth and teeth were completely blue from eating a candy push pop, and a sparkly turquoise clip held her wavy brown hair away from her face. She was growing her bangs out that summer, so barrettes and fancy clips were a must. And even though it was three o'clock, Cam still had her pajamas on: an oversized, bright green t-shirt that says *Life* in huge letters on the front, and comfy blue fleece sweatpants. It was just one of those lazy days of summer.

As she led me over to where Hunter's tree is planted, I couldn't help but feel sad. A bundle of freshly picked flowers lay on the ground in front of the perfectly shaped pine. Not long after Hunter went to heaven we were given a pine tree to plant in his honor. When we moved, the tree went with us. It stands a good five feet tall right now and seems to be thriving despite its three transplants. At the base of the tree there's a cement plaque that reads:

Your memory is our keepsake, with which we'll never part.
God has you in His keeping. We have you in our hearts.

Friends of ours who lost their infant son, Liam, to Krabbe disease gave us the memorial plaque after Hunter died. Their way of saying, "We know how you feel." Unfortunately, the plaque didn't fare as well as the tree did when we moved. It's now cracked down the middle, broken in two—like my heart.

"Look, Mommy, aren't they beautiful? I picked them in our yard," Camryn said with delight. Although she was ten years old, Cam still didn't understand that the flowers in our backyard are not meant to be picked. But for her brother, she would've picked them all.

"They're so pretty, Camryn. Thank you." I hugged her and we walked back over to the house.

———

What Camryn and Erin remember about Hunter, and what he meant and continues to mean to them, is reflected in a letter each one wrote to their beloved brother. Camryn was nine and Erin was thirteen when they journaled their tributes. Camryn completed hers first, and here's what she wrote:

My Brother Hunter
By: Camryn Kelly

I love letting balloons go up to heaven. My cousin Ben asked my mommy if balloons can really go up to Hunter. And she said, "If God wants our balloons to reach all the way up to heaven, they will. He can do whatever He wants to."

Before I let a balloon go, I put lipstick on and kiss it. Then I get a marker and write something special to Hunter on it. Usually I write, "I love you Hunter. I can't wait to see you. We miss you. Love Camryn." And then I let it go up, up, up, high in the sky. Sometimes I watch the balloon until it's only a little speck. I hope God brings our balloons to heaven. Maybe when we get to heaven we'll see all the balloons we sent to Hunter.

I miss him so much. I used to cuddle with Hunter all the time. My sister Erin and I got a new dog two years after Hunter went to heaven. Her name is Bella and she's a Chihuahua. She's the cutest little thing and I know that Hunter would've loved her because she likes to cuddle just like he did.

I miss Hunter's warm, soft skin and his smile. I miss kissing his cute face every morning and touching his wavy hair. Even though Hunter couldn't talk, we understood what he was saying. He would blink once for "yes." I loved my big brother so much and I didn't want to let him go. But I know that God had a plan for Hunter's life and He has a plan for my life too. My mommy says I look like Hunter. I like when she says that.

I remember taking baths with Hunter. My mom, Erin, Hunter, and I would have lots of fun in the Jacuzzi. One time we put bubble bath in the water and put the jets on and the bathtub overflowed with bubbles. You couldn't even see us, there were so many bubbles. Erin and I put bubbles on our heads and in our hands and blew them at Mommy and Hunter. It was hilarious.

My brother loved horses. His favorite horse was Bambi. Bambi is a chestnut brown horse, and she has a white spot on the tip of her nose and one between her eyes that looks like a star. She lives in Attica at my mommy's aunt's barn near Grammie's house. Hunter got to ride her a few times. When Hunter got bigger, my mom had to hold him sideways across Bambi's back. I was so afraid that he might fall off or that his oxygen might get disconnected. We were always very careful with Hunter. When Bambi had her baby Ohmeister, we went to visit her and she licked my mom's shoes. It was so funny. My mom always forgot to bring carrots for the horses. I haven't been to the barn to visit Bambi since Hunter went to heaven. I miss her. I wonder if Hunter misses her.

The most terrible moment in my life was when my mom, dad, and Grammie told me that Hunter went to heaven. I cried my eyes out. I didn't want it to be true. But it was. We were all crying. I still cry sometimes.

My best friend Cara had to give her dog Maisy away the other day. I felt so bad for her. She'll never see Maisy again, just like I'll never see Hunter again. But I'll see him in heaven. I wonder when that day will come. I get butterflies in my belly just thinking about it.

Hunter would always brighten up my day. I love my brother so much that sometimes I feel like my heart will explode. I wish he were still here with me, but I know that heaven is the best home for him and all of us. I wonder what he's doing there right now. I wonder what his voice sounds like and if he'll look the same. I also wonder if animals talk in heaven. That would be so cool.

I can't wait to see Hunter again. I can't wait to see Jesus. Waiting can be very hard. I sometimes wish I could go to heaven right now. But that's God decision, not mine.

Hunter was the best brother and still is, today and forever and ever. He will always have a special place in my heart.

Erin Marie had a very hard time writing her letter. She is still grieving. And although she doesn't cry or talk about her brother very often, I know she's heartbroken. I see her pain when she gets frustrated and angry for no reason. I hear the desperate cry of her heart in her silence. Here's what Erin wrote:

Thoughts from my heart . . . by Erin Kelly

I had a difficult time deciding what to write for this book. There's so much I want to say about my brother, but it's hard to describe how I feel. I miss Hunter. But I believe I will see him again. Until that day, I know living without him will be terribly hard. Hopefully I will carry the memory of his incredible life with me for as long as I live. I want to remember everything about him. He was an incredible boy, and very handsome too. I love him so much.

To express what my heart longs to say, I decided to write Hunter a letter. And through my words to him, I hope you can catch a glimpse of how much he changed my life. I'll never be the same. I miss him so much.

Dear Hunterboy,

No words can express how much I love you. There is no mountain high enough to keep me away from you. You mean more to me than anything in the entire world.

The best day of my life was when you came into my life, and the worst was when you left. I know I will see you again someday soon in eternity. But I would do anything to be with you for one more day . . . even if it was only for a second. I would do anything to touch your perfect skin or run my fingers through your curly brown hair just one last time. To watch a movie with you, play Rescue Heroes with you, and look into your handsome green eyes just one last time.

Life will never be the same without you. Home isn't home without you. Life isn't life without you. I'll never be the same. Jesus is the only reason I'm still living. I miss you more than anything.

I miss watching Davey and Goliath with you. I miss playing games with you, even though you always beat me. I miss coming home from school and knowing that there was one very important boy waiting for a hug from his big sister. I miss staring into your eyes, hoping and praying that somehow, some way I could take your place.

I know God had a reason for your suffering, even though I don't understand it all. You were put in my life for a reason. If it were not for God blessing me with you as my brother, I would be lost in this broken world.

You are a breath of fresh air. When I look at you I don't see "disabled," I see my only brother—who is very able. Because you, Hunter James Kelly, are a life changer. You changed my life without a word, and because of you, I will never ever be the same.

I can't wait to spend eternity with you.

You're the world's best brother.

I love you more than life itself!

Love, Erin

Chapter 17

Walking Through the Valley

After the girls managed to transition back to school in September, I became obsessed with busyness. Whenever idleness would rear its ugly head, I would run as fast as I could in the opposite direction. My daily agenda was completely jammed. As long as I could stay busy, it didn't matter what I was doing. I started taking theology classes every Monday night at our church through Liberty University, and I also got involved in crafting.

I decided to make bookmarks. I loved scrapbooking and had plenty of paraphernalia for the craft. So I gathered all my stickers and colorful paper and created bookmarks. The girls and I spent hours designing and laminating. We made greeting cards, too. The craft phase certainly served its purpose in occupying some of that idle time, but I remained very restless.

We celebrated my first birthday (September 9) without Hunter with little fanfare. It was a sad yet wonderful day spent with special people who meant so much to us throughout Hunter's life. Rather than bring me gifts, I had asked everyone to write their favorite memory of Hunter (see Appendix C), which immediately became greater in value and meaning than any gift I'd ever received. After I blew out the candles, we all grabbed a piece of birthday cake, handmade with love by Hunter's best friend, Robert, and his mom, Elizabeth. We then headed into the living room where, one by one, Team Hunter shared their memories. It was heart-wrenching, and we all cried a lot. Nevertheless, the joy and love in that room were unmistakable, healthy, and healing. Even reading about Hunter stirred our hearts with a fullness of joy that only God could impart. I knew I would miss our team. A lot.

Thanksgiving, Christmas, and New Year's Day 2006 came and went. Before I knew it, it was Valentine's Day (Jim's forty-sixth birthday and what would have been Hunter's ninth). Here are fragments from my journal entry for that day:

As I do every year, I decorated our house with red heart balloons, red and white streamers, confetti, and sparkles. "Happy Birthday, Daddy and Hunter" heart-shaped signs were strategically placed throughout the house. Presents wrapped in shiny red gift wrap were piled on the kitchen table, surrounded by framed pictures of Jim and Hunter. Everything looked fun and festive, ready for a day of celebrating. But all I wanted to do was grab a blanket and pillow and go to sleep in my closet where no one would find me. I didn't just want to stay in my room; I wanted to be where no one could walk in and ask me how I was. I wanted to disappear.

Jim and I went to the cemetery today. On the way there we stopped at a florist to buy a dozen red roses and two red, heart-shaped balloons.... When we arrived at the cemetery we dusted the snow off Hunter's angel. Even covered in white, she's beautiful. We tied one red balloon around the angel's wings and decided to let the other one go—up to heaven and Hunter, of course. Jim wanted to build Hunter a snowman. So we did....I brought a bag of black licorice (Jim's favorite) for the ride, so we used two pieces for his eyes and a bunch for a smiling mouth. We found a leftover blue pop-top in the backseat of the truck for the snowman's nose. A few sticks worked for arms, and Jim's red Buffalo Bills hat fit perfectly on his head. He was the cutest snowman. Imagine that—a snowman at the cemetery.

I should've been more focused on Jim today. It's his birthday. He's alive. But Hunter's not. It was so cold today. Jesus, please keep my heart from growing cold and hard during this season of grief.

Jim knows how much I love Valentine's Day, and always have (how ironic). I was shocked when he sat me down at the kitchen table this afternoon to give me a Valentine's gift. I had no idea what to expect. And I still can't believe what he said. His gift to me is that starting in March, for a half-hour every week, he will sit down with me so I can teach him about Jesus and the Bible. How cute is that. As if I'm a teacher. I wonder if it will happen. Lord, thank You for giving me hope. Thank You for showing me that You are at work in our grief.

The next few weeks passed quickly. I was convinced I was moving along in my season of mourning just fine. Except for the obvious pangs of sadness, sorrow, and sleeplessness, I imagined that everything I was experiencing was just part of the normal grief process, if there is such a thing. My grief certainly never felt normal. I never felt as though anyone was feeling the way I was. Sleep deprivation and tear-stained cheeks were old friends of mine, so when I struggled more with both, I wasn't surprised.

And then it happened. I went to bed the night of April 16, 2006, and woke up the next morning bound by a smothering gloom that paralyzed me from deep within. It was as if I had been wrapped in a shroud of emotional and spiritual darkness and cast into a bottomless abyss.

Frightened and confused, I immediately called my mother: "Mom, something's wrong with me." I was frantic. "Please come over right away."

In a few minutes she was right by my side. "I don't know what's wrong with me. My heart is racing and I feel like I'm going to have a heart attack."

She suggested we take a walk around the cul-de-sac. Erin and Camryn were busy in the playroom, so I agreed. As we walked, I talked and she listened.

During what would end up being months of severe depression, she continued to listen. Most of the time, my precious mother had no idea what to do, but she was always there. She listened. She prayed.

After our visit, my mother went into emergency mode. She contacted every prayer chain, prayer warrior, and pastor we knew. A handful of close confidants also rallied to provide encouragement and emotional support.

The heaviness of my grief was crushing. Here's my journal entry for that day.

April 17, 2006—I don't understand what's going on. I woke up this morning oppressed by a heaviness of heart I'm not familiar with. HELP ME! I'm scared to death. What is this? I feel like I've fallen into a dark abyss of depression and despair. Lord, where are You? Why do I feel so alone, abandoned? Never in all my life have I felt so downcast, so afraid, so lifeless, so damaged. My thoughts and fears overwhelm me day and night.

Save me from myself! Is this normal? I feel like a prisoner in my own flesh. I feel like every ounce of life is being choked out of me. My chest hurts and my heart won't slow down. Do You see me? Do You hear me? Please rescue me from this battle waged against me. Am I sick? I need help! Is this "the valley of the shadow of death"? My God, deliver me from this torment.

Sleep eluded me, and food had no taste. Within two weeks I had lost twenty pounds. The bold green irises of my eyes were fading to gray. With each passing day the immensity of dread and desperation grew. It got to the point where, a few times, I felt as if I would literally die from suffocation. I spent hours balled up on the floor in my closet, praying with my face buried in my Bible. I prayed through our entire house and anointed every entrance with oil. As much as possible I played worship music and recited every Scripture I had ever memorized over and over.

The LORD himself goes before [me] and will be with [me]; he will never leave [me] nor forsake [me]. [I will] not be afraid; [I will] not be discouraged.   (Deuteronomy 31:8)

The LORD will keep [me] from all harm—he will watch over [my] life; the LORD will watch over [my] coming and going both now and forevermore.   (Psalm 121:7–8)

For he will command his angels concerning [me] to guard [me] in all [my] ways.   (Psalm 91:11)[1]

As my desolation continued to intensify, doubt hammered my faith. Every time I opened up the silverware drawer in our kitchen, I wanted to grab a knife. So I stayed out of the kitchen.

Whenever I was driving alone in the truck, it took all the

strength I could muster to keep from slamming into a tree or the highway median. Eventually I was unable to drive or be alone. I had absolutely no control over the torrent of lies and fear stalking my mind, body, and spirit.

Some of my journal entries during the first month of this onslaught of depression might have easily put me in a straitjacket. This one shows how deep I had fallen, but thankfully, how great I still believed God was.

April 29, 2006—I'm going to die if You leave me here. My life is but a breath, but this is not life to me. I can't drink this cup of suffering. I can't bear the weight of this cross. I can't live like this. Come quickly, Lord, and save me. I have no one but You, and yet You seem so distant. Have I allowed a mantle of doubt to hide me from the truth? I'm crushed in spirit. Search my heart. Save me. I have nothing if I don't have You.

I knew my friends loved me and that they loved Hunter. But during the darkest months of mourning, some of the people closest to me said and did the most hurtful things. A few of my dearest friends made some suggestions they were convinced would help me in my grief: "Maybe you should consider taking down some of Hunter's pictures. You wouldn't want to make an idol or shrine out of them."

They were just trying to help, but they didn't understand. How could they? Would taking down pictures of Hunter really help me? If I packed away all the photographs, would the pieces of my heart start to mend? No. The pictures brought back wonderful memories. When I looked at them, I vividly remembered what we did that particular day and how I felt. As for making an "idol" out of Hunter, he was my son whom I loved and treasured.

Keeping the photos where they could be seen and appreciated was a reminder to me of God's goodness and love for our family.

To the left of my computer keyboard sat one of my favorite family photos. It was taken the day the Buffalo Bills retired Jim's football jersey and placed his name on the Wall of Fame at Ralph Wilson Stadium. We are walking across the football field all dressed in red, white, and blue number 12 jerseys. The picture brings back all the sights, sounds, and feelings of that unforgettable day.

The stadium was jam-packed and the roar of the fans was electrifying. As Jim and I pushed Hunter's wheelchair toward the middle of the football field where the podium stood, we could barely hear each other talk. Erin Marie was tucked in between us, and Camryn straddled my right hip. After Jim was honored, we were just about to walk off the stage when he leaned over, kissed Hunter on his forehead, and whispered, "I love you, little buddy." I knew I'd never forget the tenderness of that moment, and pictures just like this one continue to bring back such precious memories.

During this dark time, I sought help, though sometimes it didn't turn out as I had hoped. My sister-in-law, Kim, who I'm crazy about, invited me to her church for a Wednesday night service. She loves Jesus and had always been an encouragement to me. My parents were attending the same church at the time, and my mother also wanted me to come so the church elders could pray over me.

I still wasn't driving yet, so our dear friend and nanny, Jennifer, came with me. Although I listened to the message preached that night, I was anxious to be prayed over. There was an irrepressible yearning for God to move, to do something—anything. But what I experienced was far from the grace and love His children are called to extend.

After the message, my mother went up and spoke to the senior pastor of the church while Jennifer and I waited. At first I thought it was peculiar that only the senior pastor's wife made it over to where we were sitting. I assumed the elders present that evening would come, but they didn't.

Once my mom, Jen, the senior pastor's wife, and I were finally situated and only a few people remained in the sanctuary, we formed a small circle with chairs to the left of the altar. Without any sort of preparation or background as to why we were seeking prayer, the senior pastor's wife started to expound (and take out of context) some verses in the New Testament book of 2 Timothy. As she talked about weak-willed women swayed by all kinds of evil, my body shrank into the chair and my chin hit my chest. *Are you kidding me?* I thought to myself. *I'm drowning in grief and she's talking about weak-willed women. Isn't she even going to acknowledge our family's loss? Does she not recognize the avalanche of grief I am under?*

I don't remember how long she went on, but my mother eventually and graciously interrupted her and said, "I don't think you understand what's going on here." She didn't.

I wanted to escape. The last thing I remember the pastor's wife saying that night was that she thought I needed to put Jim before Hunter's Hope. I could feel myself completely unravel as we made our way out of the church. I was in shock. I had gone there for prayer and encouragement, and I was leaving discouraged and heartbroken.

Before Jen and I drove away, my mom came up to me and said in between sobs, "I'm so sorry you came here tonight, Jill. I'm so sorry. I don't understand what just happened in there, but I know God will use it. I just know it."

And she was right. But it took time and forgiveness for me to realize it.

———

Weeks passed. I continued to descend deeper into dread and what I feared was madness. Finally, we sought medical intervention in addition to the intense prayers I was already receiving.

At first I was reluctant to go to our family practitioner. My fear, rooted in pride, kept me from seeking the appropriate help I needed. However, with the encouragement of my mother, I eventually gave in. It took three visits before I was comfortable enough to start taking the antidepressant medication my doctor graciously insisted I at least try. She was incredibly patient with me.

Though it seemed like forever before my medication started to work, eventually and thankfully it did, and I began to feel better. "Better" in that I was able to function. I didn't stop crying or grieving. And I didn't walk around like a zombie or anything weird. I just felt better. It's hard to describe. (During one of my initial doctor visits my mother bluntly asked, "Is she going to walk around like a zombie if she goes on this medication?" I can laugh now when I think about how protective and bold my mother was.)

I'd never been on any sort of medication prior to this time, and even though I understood and accepted my desperate need for medical intervention, I was reluctant to tell anyone (except my mother and a close circle of friends) about the depth of what I was going through. Including Jim. I was afraid of what people would say and think. My faith had been hit so hard that the weakness of it during my darkest days was somewhat embarrassing.

While I felt let down and forsaken by some people, the sincere love and heartfelt prayers of so many others were an encouragement to me. Although few people knew the depths of my despair, those who did prayed earnestly for me and our entire family. I was so grateful for their care and generosity of spirit.

My greatest fear during those months of anguish was being separated from God. I believed the lie that I was somehow cut off from the God I believed in and loved with all my heart, soul, mind, and strength. Losing Hunter had been unimaginably dreadful, but just the thought of losing Jesus was utterly and completely devastating. He was my life. He was my hope. He was my salvation. Without Him, I knew I would never see Hunter again. And yet as deep as my despair, grief, and doubt went, He proved to be deeper still.

So while it seemed to me that my faith had failed me, Jesus hadn't. It was in pursuit of that faith that I first met my Savior, Jesus Christ. And now in Hunter's death and my grieving, that faith had been tested. In the midst of my confusion and despair, I came to realize that God was faithful, even if through the fog of depression I was unable for a time to see and connect with Him.

Slowly, ever so slowly, hope was nurtured back to life, my faith was renewed, and healing gradually began.

Chapter 18

I'm Free

Since becoming a Christian in the summer of 1998, I had been praying that Jim would also come to know Christ in a real and personal way. At that time, he told me that it didn't bother him that I turned to God for help, "but don't expect me to change, too." Still, over the next few years I witnessed simple yet profound signs that God was at work in his life.

In May 2004, for example, Jim completely surprised me for Mother's Day. He was in a rush, of course, to get out the door to catch a plane to an appearance. Before he left, though, he hurried the girls into the playroom near where Hunter and I were hanging out. And then he said, "Okay, is everybody ready?"

He motioned to the girls, and then they all started to recite Psalm 23: "The LORD is my shepherd; I shall not want. He maketh me to lie down in green pastures: he leadeth me beside the still waters..." (KJV).

I was astonished. Jim had memorized the Twenty-third Psalm for Mother's Day! For him to take the time to memorize anything other than football plays assured me that God was moving in his life. Jim explained that he had written the psalm down and placed it in various locations so that he could read it often. I couldn't believe it!

Then a few months later Jim was in Los Angeles for another appearance. He called me one afternoon while shopping with Tommy Good. "Jill," he said, "I'm in a store right now checking out some necklaces with T-Good, and I was just wondering..."

Initially I selfishly thought, *Oh brother, here we go again, like I need more jewelry.* But then Jim shocked me: "I'm checking out some of the cross necklaces, and I was just wondering what you think would be better for me—gold or silver? There are some really cool-looking crosses, too. Should I get just a simple one, or a bigger one?"

The irony of this was the fact that when I had become a Christian, one of the first things I'd done was buy a cross necklace. And here Jim was picking out a cross. Why? All I could think was that God must be doing something in Jim's heart for him to even want a cross necklace. And on top of that, he had called me to ask my opinion.

Jim had also agreed to marriage counseling. We'd been having valuable sessions with our pastor, Rich George. Counseling had begun to help us in so many ways. We really needed it. Jim and I had no idea how to communicate, much less deal with deep, hurtful issues in our relationship.

I was convinced we would get a divorce after Hunter's death. Hunter had been the glue that kept our family together.

I had been so focused on taking care of him that I didn't have time to concern myself with what Jim was doing. And what was worse, I didn't even care.

Our priorities had also been polar opposites. Mine was home. Jim's was everywhere but home...physically and mentally. From the moment we were told that Hunter was going to die, we dealt with everything completely differently. Though we never talked about it until counseling, the chasm between us had grown huge. And I had no desire to try anymore. I was just going through the motions. We were together for the kids—and then Hunter was gone. I was afraid that our marriage was gone, too. Counseling was critical (and still is).

In fact, it was during one of those sessions when our marriage came up against its greatest challenge. It was April 25, 2007. Our meeting with Pastor Rich was scheduled for eleven o'clock. We had just returned from being away together for a few days. We'd had a great time, so I imagined our session would be somewhat easy.

"I'd like for you guys to watch a video before we get started," Pastor Rich said as we all made our way into the living room. He handed me the video, I put it in, sat down next to Jim, and pushed "play."

It was a video by a well-known Bible study teacher, Beth Moore. At first I was excited because I was very familiar with Beth and loved her teaching. But I also thought it was rather odd that Pastor Rich would use Beth Moore during our counseling session. Would Jim even pay attention?

On the video Beth was talking about Joseph from the Bible, and how he had been betrayed by his brothers, sold into slavery, wrongly accused, thrown in prison, and eventually exalted to second-in-charge of all Egypt under Pharaoh. The specific Scripture Beth was discussing was Genesis 50:20: "You intended to harm me, but God intended it for good to accomplish what is now being done, the saving of many lives."

As soon as Beth recited Joseph's words, I started to cry. Those words were so familiar to me. They were words of encouragement, hope, and life. I thought of how often I had needed to remind myself of the "good" in the midst of so much suffering while caring for my beloved Hunter. The "good" that was accomplished through Hunter's Hope, the countless tears that had been wiped away, the hope that had conquered so much despair—all born as a result of my son's precious life. I missed Hunter desperately.

Pastor Rich stopped the video and asked me, "Jill, what does that mean to you right now?"

Before I could answer, I ran out of the room to get a box of tissues. After I composed myself, I sat back down and answered him: "Hunter and all the good that has come from his life. The fact that we're sitting here right now, still together, is part of the good that has come from all the pain we've been through."

It was hard to restrain the tears as I continued, "And how God has used Hunter's suffering to save me and our family. It's amazing. And what about Hunter's Hope? Children's lives are being saved because of what we're accomplishing through the foundation."

There was a momentary pause in the conversation, and then Pastor Rich looked over at Jim, who was sitting to my right, and said, "Okay, Jim, go ahead."

That's weird, I thought to myself. And then I looked at Jim. He took a deep breath, and then another one. I could tell that something was seriously bothering him. He took another deep breath and exhaled. He was very anxious about something. But what?

We had just returned from a relaxing trip together. We were getting along better than ever before. Now, as Jim sat next to me trying to compose himself, I thought something must be terribly wrong. *He's going to tell me he has cancer and has only months to live. Or maybe something's wrong with my mother and Jim needed Pastor Rich here so he could tell me.*

So many crazy thoughts bombarded my mind in those few moments that seemed to last forever. Finally, Jim tried to talk. At this point he was so emotional that tears started to pool in his eyes. When I saw them, I knew that whatever he was going to tell me was not good. Not good at all.

After inhaling deeply once again, Jim said, "This is going to be hard."

"Just take your time, Jim," Pastor Rich said.

I looked at Pastor Rich, who at this point had tears in his eyes, too. And I thought to myself, *Just tell me. What in the world is going on?*

"Um," Jim started again, followed by another deep breath. "Wow, this is a lot harder than I thought it was going to be." Then he said it: "Jill, I have not been faithful to you. For a long time, I have not been faithful. I would do okay for a little while and..."

He paused and took another deep breath. "I don't want to hurt you anymore." Another sigh.

What was I supposed to say?

I didn't know what to do.

I just sat there and stared at the coffee table in front of me.

I was shocked.

I couldn't believe what I was hearing.

"Your mother called me the day we got home from St. Kitts and told me it was very important that she see me right away. And so we met the other day, in the mall parking lot out by the girls' school. As soon as I saw her, I knew something was wrong. She handed me a letter and asked me to read it."

He paused and took another breath. "Thank God for your mother, Jill...."

My mother! How is she involved in all of this? I thought to myself. I wanted to run out of the room and call her, I was so confused and anxious.

"After reading your mother's letter, I looked at your mom and she was crying. I didn't know what to say or do. I was sort of mad and scared."

Jim paused and looked over at Pastor Rich. "Jill, I don't want to hurt you and the girls anymore. After I read your mom's letter, I wanted to change. But I needed help. I've already met with Pastor Rich, Danny, and Pastor Jerry."

As Jim continued to explain his frantic search for help, I sat there and bawled.

"Jill, I realize now that Jesus is the only one who can help me. I need Him. I don't want to lose you. I don't want to do this anymore. You don't deserve to be treated this way."

Another deep breath and he continued. "Jill, I've asked Jesus to forgive me and help me." He turned his body toward me and looked directly into my eyes as he said, "Will *you* forgive me?"

I replied, "I don't know what to say. I don't know how to feel."

I could barely look at Jim. I had given in and given up so many times. I had forgiven and started over so often I had lost count.

"I'm so thankful and yet very sad," I said as tears streamed down my face. "I'm angry but I want to be happy. What am I supposed to do?"

Hoping for some sort of guidance and encouragement, I glanced over at Pastor Rich. He was overwhelmed, too.

Jim broke the silence, looking at Pastor Rich for assurance. "Jill, everything is BC now, right, Pastor Rich?"

Caught up in a rush of raw emotions, I didn't get the "BC" comment right away.

"Yes, Jim," he said. "Everything that you have done, the mistakes and choices you've made, are forgiven. They are BC: *before Christ.* And Jill, you know that. Jim's decision to get help changes everything. When he was in my office the other day, I knew he meant business. He was desperate for help. He understood exactly what he was doing."

I wondered in that moment if Pastor Rich somehow knew what I was thinking. He knew the good, the bad, and the very ugly. During our counseling sessions over the past year I had held nothing back. He knew the vastness of the chasm that alienated Jim and me. He was privy to the sordid details of our broken, messed-up relationship.

Yet even though Pastor Rich continued to assure me of Jim's sincerity, I couldn't help feeling cynical. As much as I wanted to believe Jim, I was still doubtful. Was this just another scheme? He was a master at scrambling his way out of threatening situations; was he desperate just because he was cornered?

I was angry and hurt. I felt as if the wind had been knocked out of me.

I didn't want to wonder, but I couldn't stop myself.... *Is he sincere? Is he for real?* I wanted to believe he was telling the truth.

On numerous occasions I had prayed that God would expose Jim and bring him to a place of brokenness. And now that it had finally happened... I wasn't ready to believe it.

Not knowing exactly how to act or feel, I just sat there.

And cried.

"I feel like the weight of a piano has been lifted off my chest," Jim finally said. "I don't have to hide anymore. I don't want to hurt you anymore. And I want to play football with Hunter in heaven someday. And now I will."

Blinking back tears, Jim continued, his voice faltering, "The only word I can think of to really describe how I feel is *free*. I finally feel free."

As soon as Jim said those words, I turned toward him and whispered, "I forgive you."

When Jim said that he felt free, I knew he meant it. I knew it because that sense of freedom was familiar to me—I also knew what it meant to feel free in that way.

For Jim to finally surrender all the junk of his past was huge.

He must have felt like a new man when that crushing weight was lifted off his chest.

And of course he was. The man who had been my husband died that day. He died to himself so that he could be forgiven and set free.

In Jim's Own Words

Jacque, Jill's mother, called me and told me she needed to talk to me about something important. I had a lot going on after being out of town for a few days, so I was hoping that whatever it was wouldn't take too long.

We decided to meet in a nearby mall parking lot that morning. I pulled up next to her car, and she got out and walked over to my truck. She handed me a letter and said, "I want you to read this."

"Right now?" I asked, hoping she wasn't expecting me to read it right then and there.

"Yes, right now."

I could tell she was upset. I didn't want to read the letter while she was standing there staring at me, but I knew I had to.

"What does this mean?" I asked her once I'd skimmed it.

"I think you know what this means, Jim. You need to tell Jill."

"What?" I was frustrated and mad.

"You need to tell Jill or I'm going to."

Jacque got in her car and drove away. I pulled out of the mall parking lot and just drove. I was stunned and disoriented. As I pondered how in the world I would tell Jill, I didn't even notice that a school bus had stopped to let some kids off on the opposite side of the road in front of me. I slammed on the brakes and sat there in shock. As soon as I could, I pulled off to the side of the road and started reading through Jacque's letter again.

In the letter Jacque said she knew that I was still living an immoral lifestyle, and she could not just sit by and let my behavior destroy Jill and the girls. She said she wanted to believe that I still loved Jill, but if that was true, I needed to acknowledge the bondage I was trapped in, confess everything to Jill, and ask her and Jesus for forgiveness. Her last words were, "Humble yourself before God. He already knows everything. He is waiting. Let Him free you, Jim." She would be praying that God would open my eyes and heart.

As I read through the letter, I knew I needed help. I was afraid of what Jill might do when she found out. This wasn't the first time I had screwed up. Would she forgive me again? And of course, I thought about the girls. I didn't want to lose them, too. I had caused such a mess.

After I finished reading the letter I immediately called my brother Danny. I got his voice mail and left a message, telling him I needed to talk to him as soon as possible. And then I called Pastor Rich. I couldn't get ahold of him either.

Danny eventually called me back and assured me that he would be there for me. Dan contacted Pastor Rich and set up a meeting at church that afternoon. The three of us met, and I told them everything and then we prayed. I don't remember my exact words, but I remember how I felt after I prayed: like a huge weight had been lifted off of me. The feeling was like nothing I had ever experienced in my life. I wish I had known before what it was like to trust Jesus; I would have done it a long time ago.

The following day I had a meeting with Jill's mom and dad at Pastor Rich's office. I had asked Pastor Rich to call Jacque and Jerry for me to ask them to meet. I needed to talk to them face-to-face. I wanted them to know that I was sorry.

I was a nervous wreck, but I felt like everything would be okay. Jill's dad, Jerry, is like a brother to me. Jerry and Jacque had forgiven me before, so I was hoping they would again.

After we all sat down I didn't really know what to do or say. I couldn't wait to get out of there, and at the same time I was sort of excited to share the good news about Jesus. Pastor Rich looked at me, and I looked over at Jill's parents and said, "I know that you've heard me say this before, but not since Jesus. I'm sorry for what I did to Jill. I'm sorry. I screwed up and I'm sorry. And I finally realize that in order for this to stop, I need help. I need Jesus."

Jerry had his head down while I was talking, and as soon as I stopped, he looked up at me, "I've heard you say that before, Jim. This is my daughter we're talking about. What would you do if it were your daughter? How would you feel if someone did this to Erin or Camryn?"

I don't remember what everybody said that day, but I remember what Jerry said and how I felt afterward. I have been blitzed and sacked by 250-pound linebackers that resembled pick-up trucks more than people, and they hadn't hit as hard as Jerry's words. I can't even imagine what I would do if someone hurt my girls. It wouldn't be good, I know that much.

When the meeting was over, Jacque gave me a hug. I'll never forget that hug. She cried a lot during our meeting.

Before I left, Pastor Rich asked me if I wanted him to be there for me when I told Jill, and of course I did.

The next day was our meeting. I just wanted to get it over with. I was so nervous, not knowing what Jill would say or do when she found out. I had been praying throughout the night *that she would forgive me. And I was thinking a lot about Erin and Camryn. I didn't want to hurt them.*

After we sat down and watched a short video with Pastor Rich, it was my turn to talk. I had a very hard time and didn't want to look at Jill because she kept crying. Even though what I had to say was really bad, I also had the greatest news ever to share. I guess I was hoping that the good would outweigh the bad. I was hoping that Jill would forgive me. And she did. I could tell that she wasn't sure whether to believe me or not, though. And I don't blame her for that. I would never have put up with me if I were her. I still can't believe she forgave me.

"You both have a long road ahead," Pastor Rich said. "You're both very different people now. And Jim, now you have Christ to help you every step of the way."

After all was said and done, as we stood up to walk Pastor Rich to the front door, Jill gave me a hug. I don't ever remember feeling the way I did when she gave me that hug.

I needed her forgiveness.

I'll never forget it.

It felt like I was floating.

I felt forgiven.

And I felt free.

Chapter 19

Forever

It was September 19, 2008, the day Jim and I were to renew our wedding vows. As I got ready, I was overwhelmed. I thanked the Lord for His generosity, for loving Jim and me enough to keep us together, and for His forgiveness, restoration, hope, and healing. I prayed that He would prepare our hearts—all of us: Erin and Camryn, all the guests, Jim, me, Pastor Rich, the whole crew— and that God would be glorified in every part of the day.

We spent the entire day preparing. Jim had the guys setting up tables and chairs while the girls addressed the fine details of the event. My maid of honor and best friend from high school, Karyn, made sure, as she always does, that every detail was nailed down. After years of telling me that I was crazy for staying with Jim, Karyn was there for me. Her excitement and commitment to this extraordinary occasion meant so much to me—even though she still thought I was crazy and made sure she told me so one more time.

Finally, everything was ready. Hunter's Haven Lodge had been completely transformed into a woodsy fairy-tale land. The open pavilion overlooking Two Sisters Pond (named after Erin and Camryn) was draped with cream-colored silk and white sheen tulle that pooled on the pebble stone floor. An elaborate candle pillar altar made a picturesque backdrop where Jim and I would renew our marriage commitment. Hundreds of vanilla votive candles wrapped in gold glitter lined the center aisle and lit up the entire place, while pale white rose petals lay sprinkled around the covered guest chairs. Though there was a slight chill in the evening air, the candles brought welcomed warmth to the pavilion, so serene and beautiful in the soft moonlight.

As our guests filled the seats, I scurried around the main lodge getting ready. In contrast to our wedding, I wanted to simplify as much as possible. I kept my hair and make-up understated, with Erin Marie making sure I didn't overdo. And except for one thing—the fairy-tale princess skirt from my wedding—I pulled my outfit together with clothes from my closet. I had decided to wear that one part of my original wedding dress because the detachable silk tulle overskirt was still as beautiful as it was the first time I wore it. Oddly, I had always hoped to wear that piece of my dress again. It was so spectacular I thought maybe even Erin or Camryn might choose to wear it when they got married.

The last thing I had to do before mounting my camouflage golf-cart-chariot was put on the tulle skirt. Everything else was done. My mom finished ironing it and handed it to me. As I talked through how I imagined the events of the evening would proceed, thirteen-year-old Erin Marie, who was close by listening, politely interrupted me and asked, "Mommy, do you think I can say something tonight at your ceremony?"

I was so surprised. "Oh my, Erin! Of course you can. I didn't ask you because I thought you would be nervous talking in front of all those people. We would love it."

In the midst of all the hustle and bustle, I found myself reflecting on some of the events that had led up to this moment. I thought about how incredible it was that Jim and I had survived. We were different now. Everything had changed. It was almost as if we were getting married for the very first time.

We had been through so much. We had wanted to give up and walk away many times. Yet we didn't.

Divorce was no longer lurking around the corner of our lives. Unforgiveness and deception had no part in our relationship anymore. Unconditional love had healed our broken and hardened hearts. After twelve years of marital strife, we had finally discovered what real love was. We were now truly in love—possibly for the first time ever—for real. It was incredible.

It was a miracle.

"Mom, can you believe this is really happening?" I said as I grabbed my perfectly ironed skirt from her hands.

"Only God, Jill...only God," she responded.

As I pulled the tulle overskirt up over my hips and draped the silk bow across my waist to fasten the hidden buttons, I paused. While everyone in the room stared at me, patiently waiting to gaze upon the finished product—I burst out laughing.

"It doesn't fit." I laughed.

"You've got to be kidding me," my mother replied. "Didn't you try it on?"

"No. I knew the other piece of the dress would never fit me, but I thought for sure the skirt would. What are we going to do?" I exclaimed.

"Do you even have a sewing kit here?" my mother asked as she started rifling through the bathroom drawers.

"I have no idea. I doubt it."

I started laughing again, and my mother and Karyn joined me.

How appropriate that in the midst of these intense preparations and heart-pondering moments, a bit of comic relief should intrude. I had managed to keep back tears all day long, and now, ironically, as I started to really think about all that was happening, *my skirt didn't fit.* How perfect. I was rather thin for our wedding, but I didn't think I had gained that much weight. It must have been the three kiddos.

I don't remember where the needle and thread came from or how my mother managed to move the buttons and sew them back on, but she did. And it was hysterical.

At 7:30 p.m., as the sun started to set over the scenic Ellicottville hills, my camouflage chariot was ready.

"Do I look okay?" I said to my mother.

"You look beautiful, Jill."

As my "entourage" and I slowly made our way down the stairs, my dad was waiting patiently at the bottom. He looked so handsome and happy. I love my dad; we had been through so much together.

Through the years my dad had watched me deteriorate in despair and defeat and then rise up with courage and hope. He had witnessed the transformation of our entire family. And though he said very little, I knew he was amazed that we had all come so far.

I could hear the soft beautiful piano music playing in the distance as I carefully slid into the golf cart. My mother, camera in hand, joined us.

I was so nervous.

My dad drove us down to the pavilion nestled between Hunter's Cabin and Two Sisters Pond. As we parked, cameras flashed like lightning all around us. Camryn and Paige, my six-year-old niece, sprinkled the ground with rose petals while my nephew Ben kept my skirt from dragging along the ground. As my dad and I made our way down the candlelit aisle toward Jim and Pastor Rich, there was a heavenly hush throughout the pavilion. I tried not to make eye contact with anyone because I knew if I did, I would lose it.

We had purposefully invited everyone who was there. Jim and I wanted an intimate ceremony. We wanted to share this very meaningful event with special people: Individuals who had walked beside us through the many tumultuous seasons of our marriage. Friends who were at the party the night I met Jim in 1991. Family members who had watched us grow apart and struggle for years. Dear friends who came to our rescue when life started to crumble. Those who loved us and spent countless hours praying for our entire family. We wanted to share this deeply cherished night with these treasured few.

Everyone there needed to see the answer to years of prayer. They needed to stand witness to the fact that the impossible is possible.

As we stood with Pastor Rich, the glow of hundreds of candles lit the area and a gentle breeze swayed the elegant draping back and forth. It seemed as if time actually stood still. Initially, Pastor Rich cracked a few simple jokes to lighten the mood and calm our hearts. Jim and I were both nervous. Not so much because we were standing in front of our friends, but because of why we were there.

I hadn't written down what to say to Jim; instead, we decided to spontaneously share what was on our hearts. A simple ceremony of prepared words just wouldn't do this time.

The expression of our commitment to love each other no matter what had to be real. I wanted the intimacy and intensity of what we were about to do to echo in our hearts into eternity— and in the minds and hearts of all who were there to share the event with us.

To start off the ceremony, our two nephews, Benjamin and Zac, and our daughter Camryn each read a Scripture from the

New Testament. Then Bill and Mooch, two longtime family friends, each made their way up to the microphone to say a few words. Mooch glanced over at us and began, "I am amazed when I think back on how Jim and Jill's marriage started. We saw a beautiful, blonde, green-eyed Jill from 'our little Attica' marrying a big, popular football star, Jim. You might say they both *found the right person*. It was a fairy tale come true!

"What I see now is a spiritually beautiful Jill and Jim. What I think we all need to understand is that marriage is not about *finding* the right person. Marriage is about *being* the right person. Praise God that, in Christ, Jill and Jim are new creations. They now bear the fruit of righteousness—love...joy...peace...patience...kindness...goodness...faithfulness...gentleness...and self-control—that will allow them to *be the right person.*

"I feel that what these two have now is far better than any 'fairy tale come true'! I am so thankful to be a part of such a special evening, and I look forward to growing together with them and their family in Christ."

My dear friend Mary got up to share after Mooch. Her words were mixed with tears and fell on our hearts.

When Erin Marie started to share, I could barely control the flood of emotions welling up inside me. Her eloquence and tenderhearted reverence for Jim and me was incredibly moving. Here's what she said:

Dear Mom and Dad...

Mom, my life would not be the same without you. You have taught me that with God all things are possible. Without you, I don't know what I would do. You have been there for me when I felt like there was never going to be a tomorrow. You were there through the stomachaches and the tears, through the bad dreams and the mistakes.

Dad, words cannot express the way I feel about you. I remember writing a report about you for school. I remember going to basketball practice and my basketball games with you and going to football games with you. I remember you telling me to block out and take electrolyte strips that I thought tasted disgusting. Even though I don't always want to practice, thank you for pushing me to do it. You are the greatest dad. You had many fans cheering you on during your football career. You were their hero. Daddy, you're always my hero, always and forever.

Mom and Dad, today as you renew your wedding vows, I believe that you are making a confession of faith. Today you are standing in front of your friends and family, showing them that you are renewing your wedding vows because you are both now children of the Lord. You are showing your peers that, even now, after all you have been through, God is love and He is in control. And the verse I chose for you today is 1 Corinthians 13:4–8, 13: "Love is patient, love is kind. It does not envy, it does not boast, it is not proud. It is not rude, it is not self-seeking, it is not easily angered, it keeps no record of wrongs. Love does not delight in evil but rejoices with the truth. It always protects, always trusts, always hopes, always perseveres. Love never fails. . . . And now these three remain: faith, hope and love. But the greatest of these is love."

I love you, Mom and Dad.

There wasn't a dry eye in the pavilion.

Love certainly was in the air that evening. More than a love between family and friends. More than a love between a newly committed husband and wife. Love even bigger than that of a mother and father for their treasured, one and only son.

We were drawn to the gravity of a love greater and deeper than our love, pain, and sorrow. A love more profound. We'd tasted this love in the face of suffering and were now compelled to share it with anyone and everyone. A love that is patient and kind, longsuffering and never failing. A love between a Father and His Son. Love beyond comprehension. Love that conquers all. And though love was exchanged in many ways that evening, it was the love spoken without a word that changed everything.

———

Clearly, we didn't have it all figured out then, and we still don't. We're on a marriage journey for life that continues to need constant prayer. But here's the important thing: we are not the same people anymore. While it didn't happen overnight, our family was changed and we're on a totally different program now, following a new playbook for life. And it's incredible.

Jim and I have absolutely no desire to go back to that old life filled with selfishness and betrayal. We didn't come to this place in our journey by chance. We never determined to live for each other rather than ourselves by our own efforts. Our lives were so saturated in sin and self-indulgence that only a divine work of God could have rescued us. And it did. God made us desperate for Him—and in that desire for Him, He gave us our marriage back, better than it ever was, stronger than it ever could have been. If not for love, I'm certain Jim and I would've divorced. Because of love, we'll never be the same.

In Jim's Own Words

I have to admit, the idea of renewing our vows was Jill's. I always thought people did this when they were in their fifties or sixties. After talking it through, however, it made sense for us to go before God and renew our marriage commitment again. At our first wedding, neither of us really understood the magnitude of what it meant to be committed. I know I didn't. Everything was so different then. We were both different. And then everything changed when Hunter got sick. Our love for him and our two girls kept us together until we both realized our need for God.

Our renewal was about more than just our vows. It was the coming together of our hearts. What was broken in the past had been mended, and we wanted to express to everyone and to each other how much that meant and the seriousness of it.

Marriage is hard. It is. Jill and I still need help, but now we have Christ. I may not be as outwardly expressive about my faith as Jill is, but I know who saved our marriage, our family, and our future.

To think that in eight and a half years, God had been working His plan through the life of a helpless little boy who never spoke a single word, but nonetheless completely altered a family's life for eternity is, well . . . indescribable.

Chapter 20

The Time in Between

One of my favorite Bible passages is Ecclesiastes 3:1–8. It begins, "There is a time for everything, and a season for every activity under heaven: a time to be born and a time to die, a time to plant and a time to uproot"...and so on. You may have read or heard these verses before and noticed that the author of Ecclesiastes compared contrasting experiences—experiences that have a period of time in between them. The time between birth and death. The time between our weeping and our laughter. The time between searching and giving up, keeping and throwing away, war and peace...and between mourning and dancing.

After more than four years of living without Hunter, it hasn't gotten any easier. So far, my time in between—my time between mourning and dancing—has been characterized by an agonizingly slow process of grieving. After Hunter's death I heard people say, "The first year is the hardest." I disagree. Every day without Hunter has been hard—every day. I wish I could run away from the expectations of grief and sorrow. I've been told, "It will get better." Maybe it will, but I can't say that because I haven't experienced the "better" yet. My arms still ache to hold my boy.

Everything has changed.

Everything is different.

And yet Christ's sustaining love remains the same.

People say, "As time goes by, you will heal." Why do people set a timetable for grief? If time heals, that would mean that as time goes by, the pain eventually goes away.

The pain doesn't go away.

It doesn't.

I live with it every day.

But I still live. I still have joy. I still find pleasure in a cup of coffee in the morning and a night out at the movies. I smile and laugh with my daughters and snuggle with my husband. But the pain is still there.

And it always will be.

Should I expect it to go away? Pain is an unlikely companion. It continues to remind me that I'm still alive. I'm still a wife and mother of three precious children. Oddly, my sorrow helps keep me focused on what really matters. It keeps me humble and grounded. It continues to remind me that I'm a stranger in a strange land—I'm not home yet!

I've often wondered what life would be like without heartbreak. What if I woke up tomorrow morning and everything was better? What would it be like? It's almost impossible to comprehend, but I think life void of heartbreak is self-centered and loveless. Love is what drives my sorrow. If I hadn't loved Hunter so much, I wouldn't ache with longing right now. If I didn't love him so much, the anguish of his absence would've dissipated by now. If God didn't love me so much, maybe He would've never blessed me with a sick son.

Time doesn't heal; it just goes by. God heals. And He chose not to heal Hunter this side of eternity. I don't understand why. But I am convinced that He knew what was and still is best for Hunter, Jim, the girls, and me.

Maybe we needed to be healed more than Hunter did. What if Hunter's disease wasn't a tragedy but a triumph somehow? What we perceived as evil (surely, disease is evil), God used for good.

Could it be that in my brokenness I was healed? What if the healing I was so desperately searching for could only be found at the end of this road of brokenness and despair—at the end of myself? I don't know. But as I continue to live and breathe and grieve, I ponder these things in my heart. What's a grieving mommy to do? Some well-meaning people have said to me: "God will never give you more than you can handle." Well, missing Hunter is way more than I can handle—way more. At times, just getting out of bed has been more than I could handle.

God knew I couldn't handle watching my son slowly die. I was steeped in anguish, and everything in me apart from my mother's heart wanted to run away and never come back. God knew I would feel helpless and hopeless living without my only son. Maybe that's why He sent His Son—because He knew I couldn't handle it. If I could, I wouldn't need Jesus.

Here's another cliché I've heard from time to time: "He's in a better place." Of course he's in a better place: he's in heaven. But I'm not there yet. I'm still here. All of Hunter's things are still here. But he's not. He's gone and it seems like forever since I touched his precious face. Heaven seems so far away. Hunter seems so far away. As each day goes by, I have to remind myself that every day is one day closer to heaven, to Hunter, to home, to Jesus.

There's no twelve-step program or secret healing remedy for mourning. It's just not that easy, nor should it be. Grief spits in the face of routine and self-sufficiency. It makes a mockery of comfort and complacency and pierces your heart when you least expect it. At first it seems like a journey with a final destination, but then sometimes you find yourself back where you started, experiencing the loss again and again.

Grief is so unlike anything—almost as if it is unnatural and just doesn't belong. And it's such a lonely place. Strangers are not welcome there, and friends usually don't stay very long.

Inevitably we all experience grief, and we all grieve differently. And it's okay. It has been a hard lesson, but eventually I realized that Jim and I would always deal with the loss of our son very differently. More than four years after Hunter's death, we are just now finally beginning to talk to each other about our grief.

We've been taking walks together in our neighborhood lately. I tease Jim that he's getting old and can't really keep up with me anymore, so I have to walk circles around him in order to get any sort of exercise. He insists that his labored stride is due to all those hits he endured while being the toughest quarterback in the NFL. But it's okay that he can't keep up because we talk during our walks, and that is huge. Honestly, I'll drag him around our neighborhood in a little red wagon if I have to. Whatever it takes to continue having the conversations we've been having lately, I'll do it.

For the first time in our marriage, we are talking about things never discussed before—out-of-comfort-zone topics, failures, and wounds of the past. You name it, we are bringing it up.

On one particular day in late summer 2009, Jim and I were walking and discussing possible subtitle ideas for this book.

"Let's just think of words, simple words that describe Hunter and our story," I suggested.

"Courage and bravery...how one child changed the world," Jim offered.

"What about hope and love?" I responded as I circled Jim... again. "Our entire story and Hunter's life is a love story. It's all about love, don't you think? So how does this sound...*Without a Word: A Family's Love Story*?"

As we reached the end of the cul-de-sac on our street, Jim

replied, "What about *Without a Word: Our One and Only Son?* How about that? That sounds sort of biblical because our one and only son brought us to God's one and only Son. And you always say that, Jill, right?"

He's right, I do. I'm amazed by the parallels between our love for Hunter and God's love through Christ. It inspires me to press on every day.

Jim and I continued to walk and talk, and after a while I brought up a subject we'd prayed about and considered but up to that point had decided not to pursue: "So, have you thought any more about adopting?"

Without hesitation Jim responded, "Nope. HB's my boy, and I'm glad he was chosen to be my one and only son. He's my son, and he's the best."

Whatever God was doing in Jim's heart became even more evident to me in those moments. We had both wanted to adopt and had thoroughly researched our options, but we eventually realized that our motives were rooted in selfishness. Jim had wanted a healthy son. So did I. Though adoption would have been great, it would not have healed our hearts. We both needed to come to a place where we were content with what was. We needed to know that adopting a boy would never fill the tremendous void that Hunter left. Only God could help us to surrender our desires so that we could learn to be thankful that our son, Hunter . . . would be our one and only son.

I slowed my pace so I could walk right next to my husband. "Jim, do you see how God has worked this all out for good? It's incredible."

"Yeah, we wouldn't even be here right now. Everything would be different. But here we are, exactly where Hunter would want his mommy and daddy to be, together and in love."

We were also exactly where *we* wanted to be. Yet like the

writer of Ecclesiastes, we also recognized that we were living in a time in between. A time in between saying good-bye to Hunter and seeing his beautiful face again. The period when everything rides on hope as we trust and cling to the Keeper of the unseen.

When we finished our walk that day and returned home, I thought some more about the question, "What about the time in between?" And I've thought about it a lot since that summer day. I understand that there is a tender balance in living with one foot here on Earth while the other desperately longs to step from time into eternity.

I know I'm not home yet. There is life all around me and I am still alive. I'm a wife and a mother...I have so much to live for, and yet my heart longs for heaven—for my forever home. I am still torn between living with the loss of a beloved child and surrendering to the Father's will. It's a daily struggle to trust that everything will be okay in this time in between.

I also understand that my time in between ultimately depends on the reality of the unseen. It was during my darkest moments of smothering despair that the faith and hope I clung to proved to be a mighty, impenetrable fortress. And the absolute certainty of what I do not see, sustained by the promises kept for me through my salvation, are carrying me through the in-between time, and will sustain me until time is no more. Although I don't know what the future holds, it is clear to me who holds the future.

Knowing that changes how I live and love.

It changes how I celebrate.

And how I grieve...

Yes, I've had to acknowledge to myself that even after four years, I am still grieving. I have discovered that while there are some things in life you can find a way around, grief is not one of them. I have found no way around it, only a way through.

My journey of grief has been unique in many ways, but one

event in my life while Hunter was still alive is proving particularly significant in allowing me to further work through it.

When Hunter was six years old, I had a very vivid dream about him. There were four people in my dream: Hunter, Jim, my girlfriend Mary, and me. Hunter and I were in a large room that was unfamiliar to me. After finishing Hunter's chest therapy, I got up and walked out of the room and down a hall. As I turned around and started to make my way back toward the room where I'd left Hunter, there he was down the hall, walking toward me. He was walking, and he looked right at me, but didn't say anything.

Typical of a dream, everything was in slow motion. As soon as I saw Hunter, I ran toward him and scooped him into my arms. I was crying and calling out to Jim, "Jim, Hunter's healed! You have to come here right away! Hunter's healed! He's healed!" I looked down at Hunter, and he just looked up at me and didn't say a word. I yelled down the hall for Jim again. "Jim, Hunter can walk! He can walk!"

Jim finally heard me and yelled back, "That's great, Jill. I've got to get going or I'll be late for my appearance. I'll talk to you later."

I was shocked and bothered by his response, so I quickly called my friend Mary. Hunter was now sitting next to me on the bed, staring at me and still not saying a word. I stood up and started pacing back and forth while holding the phone to my ear. As soon as Mary answered the phone, I exclaimed, "Mary, you're not going to believe this. Hunter's healed! He's okay! He can walk!"

"Wow, that's amazing, Jill. Hey, did I tell you about the new gift we have right now at Estée Lauder?"

And then, just like that, my dream ended.

I thought and prayed about my dream for days and asked God to help me understand its meaning. And He did.

Here's what I believe God wanted me to understand... *people forget*. If God had healed Hunter this side of heaven, people would eventually forget. Initially, the shock and excitement of Hunter walking and talking, playing and smiling would be huge news—the top medical story everywhere, maybe even globally. However, it would only be a matter of time before something new would come along and people would forget.

We would all move on to the next big story. And the miracle would become yesterday's news. That's just the way we are.

As meaningful to me as that dream was when Hunter was alive—and however profound the lesson learned—I now believe there is another, perhaps even more significant, meaning that could only have been revealed after Hunter's death. True, Hunter's physical healing would have been pronounced a "miracle." And indeed it would have been. But the miracles that are at the heart of the life and death of Hunter James Kelly are so much more profound than a single miracle of healing: The miracle of my marriage surviving. The miracle of our family still being together. I see a miracle every time I look at my two precious daughters and recognize the emotional and spiritual maturity brought about by their lives with Hunter. Hunter's Hope Foundation is a miracle, and so are the lives being touched by the work there.

But the most profound miracle of all was having my son's suffering lead me, Jim, and our two girls to the greatest act of suffering that changed (and continues to change) everything—the Cross of Christ. In understanding His sacrifice and suffering, we have found meaning and beauty in Hunter's suffering.

So now, during this time in between earth and heaven, we cling to the one Person we desperately need, because He, too, is acquainted with sorrow and grief. The joy and hope in knowing that inspires us to persevere as we anticipate tomorrow, treasure yesterday... and look forward to forever.

Epilogue

While I Wait

September 9, 2009

I'm sitting in my office looking around at the clutter that follows writing a book—journals, memoirs, notes, reminders, my Bible, page after page of words—and my eyes wander out the window. I see the beauty of the first signs of autumn everywhere. Fall is my favorite season, and always has been. After all, it's when... football season starts! ("Are you ready for some football?" We are always ready for some football in the Kelly house.) The sprawling sunburst honey locust tree outside my window is starting to turn a stunning array of golden yellow hues. And our maple trees are changing, bursting into all sorts of maroon, red, and bright orange shades. It's breathtaking.

Today is my birthday. I turn thirty years old...okay, forty. Jim, Erin, and Camryn woke me up this morning with snuggles and singing. The birthday hat Camryn insisted I wear is just a tad tight—kind of like some of the cute jeans I used to wear. I'm surprised my little Chihuahua didn't come running through the house with a party hat on, too. It's probably only a matter of time before Camryn makes me beat a piñata or do something equally embarrassing. I mean, I am forty.

Regardless of the fact that all three of them would like to see me run around like a monkey and perform circus tricks, I do know they love me and want me to have fun today. The number forty is plastered all around the kitchen, thanks to Jim and his two little helpers. I get it . . . I'm forty, and you want everyone and their brother to know it.

Before bed last night Jim prayed, "Lord, please bless Mommy now that she's over the hill." Very funny! After he finished praying and before Erin started, I gasped, "Wait a minute, I thought the over-the-hill thing was for when you turn fifty, not forty."

Jim smiled and laughed. "Oh yeah, you're right."

He'll turn fifty in less than six months. I've got him by ten years (actually, only nine as of today)—but I'll always be younger and will never stop reminding him.

As Cam was leaving for school this morning she begged me to dance the limbo under one of the decorative, sparkly fortieth-birthday things hanging in our kitchen. (You thought I was kidding about the circus acts.) Reluctantly, I did the limbo. I did it over and over and over again. Camryn and I laughed the laugh that hurts your stomach and makes your jaw sore.

Before she walked out the door she grabbed both my arms and said, "Mom, I need to give you forty kisses before I leave, four real ones and one in the air for the zero in forty." Of course, we kissed four times and once to the air between our two faces. She is such a cool kid! Her personality liberates my soul.

She ran out the door, but after a few seconds burst back in after forgetting her drink for school. Jim was beeping the horn because he hates being late. I should have gone outside and made him do the limbo. . . .

It was another typical morning at the Kelly household.

Or was it?

Exactly a year ago today we signed papers to buy the house we now live in, the house Jim and I still can't believe we own. After we moved, a few of my friends asked me how the transition went. I guess they assumed it would be hard to leave the house all three of our children grew up in; the house that Hunter lived in his entire life. Oddly and thankfully, the transition was incredibly smooth. I don't miss our old house at all—evidence that God is still at work in healing my broken heart.

So today is my fortieth birthday.

And it's been 1,496 days since I held Hunter's hand, looked into his gorgeous green eyes, and told him, "I love you, little buddy." It's been that long since he raised his cute eyebrows and blinked back three times. But I'm also 1,496 days closer to seeing his beautiful face again, to hearing him talk for the first time and feeling him wrap his arms around my neck.

The gift of Hunter's life will continue to astound me for as long as I live. Through Hunter, God made death a fearless passage. He taught us to look to our next life with a longing that only He can bestow. We have an eternity with Hunter waiting for us.

Every passing day is one day closer to that glorious reunion. One day closer to heaven. One day closer to the One who paints the stars in the sky and teaches the sparrows how to fly. The One who holds me right now and waits to hold me for forever.

So I celebrate and cry today. Not because I'm no longer in my thirties, but because I'm here. The yearning I have for heaven has to balance out the yearning I have to stay in this temporary life and be the best mother and wife I can be. I have an amazing family and great friends. These people all deserve to see my zest for life—this beautiful gift of life on earth that I have with them. I pray that my joy and hopes for tomorrow are reflected in my relationships today.

Wait…how can I have a passion for anything at all when my boy isn't here? He's gone. But tomorrow I will be 1,497 days closer to him, remember? It baffles the mind, but I know it's true. I want every single minute of my life to count for something greater than I can fully comprehend, as Hunter's did.

The question before me is, "What will I do with the time I have left, knowing that every breath is a gift?"

Will I cry sometimes? Absolutely. Will I want to hide in bed some mornings? Probably. Will I possibly dance around and do the limbo to make my children laugh so that I can laugh? Of course I will. But it's all right because everything's going to be okay—right now and forever. Plain and simple…I was blind but now I see.

Jim has a birthday dinner planned for tonight with my family, and he better not try to pull a surprise party or anything. It's not that I don't like surprises; I just want to know about them before they happen. I was the little girl who searched the house to find hidden Christmas presents, and if they were wrapped when I found them, I carefully opened them and peeked anyway.

I guess I have a hard time waiting for what I know is going to be great. So like Christmas morning, I wait to experience the indescribable gift of being on the other side of time, in eternity.

Later today I'm going to spend the afternoon with my mother, sorting through the thousands of photos we have of Hunter. We plan to pick out just the right ones for this book. And as we look at each picture, we'll probably cry and laugh and cry some more.…And that's exactly how I want to spend this day: remembering my son and all that God did through his brief and incredible life.

Because I'm missing the boy whose unspoken love…

Changed everything…

Without a word.

Acknowledgments

There are many special people who deserve praise for having been instrumental in making this memoir a reality. People I met as a result of journeying through this project, and individuals who've been there with me all along.

You all mean so much to me—more than I can possibly describe or explain. I thank God for all of you and your partnership with me in bringing this heart-engraved work to fruition. You're amazing people. What a blessing it is to have you all in my life. Thank you for everything!

To the entire FaithWords team: Joey Paul, wow. You have gone above and beyond. I'm truly overwhelmed by all you have done to polish this heart-drenched memoir. You have invested much, and we are deeply grateful. To your precious wife, Sharon: I thank God for the blessing of having your eyes and heart touch this, too. To Holly Halverson, Whitney Luken, and the rest of the team: I'm thankful for the privilege of working with you. We have entrusted our story, our testimony, into your hands, and we're so glad we did.

To Kris Bearss: I'm so thankful that God allowed you to play such an important role in the editing process of *Without a Word*.

God will use the time and talent you have poured into this memoir in ways we can't even imagine; of this I am certain. Thank you for everything, Kris.

To the "Pray for Jill Kelly" Facebook Prayer Team: Thank you for your commitment to pray our family through this bookwriting journey. I felt the power of your countless prayers on my behalf every time I sat down at my computer. And I continue to pray that God will bless you in ways only He can. And to Katherine McCauley, my dear friend who started the Facebook Prayer Team: You will never know how thankful I am for your commitment to stand in the gap for me. Thank you for rallying prayer warriors and for being one yourself. Without you, I'd never be able to make the best meatloaf in the whole world—and I'd never know the blessing of sharing life with such a wonderful friend.

To Robert Wolgemuth and the entire staff at Wolgemuth & Associates (affectionately known by the Kelly family as "Team Wolgemuth"): Your encouragement has meant so much to me. What you do is more than a profession—it's a calling, and I've witnessed the hand of God use each one of you in such profound ways. Erik: Thank you for being an excellent Publishing 101 instructor. Michael: Thanks for your passion and excitement. What an encouragement you (and your precious wife) have been. Robert: Thank you for your friendship and for believing in the author I didn't know I could be. This book and its powerful message are a testimony of your faith in the One who made it all possible. Please give Bobbie a hug for me...she's fabulous.

To Tim McGraw and Faith Hill: Your willingness to be involved in our memoir in such a profound way blows us away. Thank you so much! Your love for each other and your commitment to family are an example to all of us. You remind us to *live like we're dying.*

To Nancy Guthrie: Thank you for your words of encouragement. Your experience and wisdom in the literary world have been invaluable to me. I look forward to meeting Hope and Gabe someday. What a day that will be.

To Rick Kern, otherwise known as Maverick or Barney (short for Barnabas—Son of Encouragement): You, my dear friend and confidant, are a writer's dream—especially a writer who never knew she could actually write. I don't want to be on a team or fight a battle unless I know you're going to be there, too. I can't imagine writing anything unless I know you'll be the first to get your hands on it. You're an amazing writer, meticulous editor, super dad, gracious brother, and treasured friend. I thank my God every time I remember you...and I always will. Get some sleep.

To Patti Thomas: Are you kidding me? Can you believe we met when we were just thirteen years old and we're still going strong? Patti, you are so talented. Thank you for dropping everything to take a good, long, hard look at *Without a Word*. I appreciate every tear you have cried to help make this memoir what it is.

To Team Hunter: From the depths of my heart I love you. We all miss you terribly. You're family, and you always will be. Not a day goes by that I don't think about our beloved Hunterboy, and not a day goes by that he's not cheering each and every one of you on from the mighty grandstands of heaven. We will see him again, girls (and Robert, Justin, and Jaden)...we will. And when we do, let's reunite the Hopesters and have a prayer party, too.

To the Hunter's Hope Families: What a blessing it is to know you and share this most difficult journey with you. You are loved. There will be a grand reunion in heaven someday. I can hardly wait.

To our dear friends and ambassadors: You know who you are. Your companionship, confidence, love, and sincere desire to see our family rise above the heartbreak and devastation will never be forgotten. I love you and thank you for praying us through. P.S. Keep praying.

To my husband, Jim: To think that you and I have come this far...wow. I love you, Jim, and I always will. You may have been one of the toughest quarterbacks to play the game, but you were vulnerable enough to share this writing journey with me. Thank you so much for opening your heart and supporting me so eagerly. God has been so good to us. Thank you for walking through life with me. If I had the chance to do it all over again...I'd still pick you.

To my girls, Erin and Camryn: God must have been thinking about me when He made both of you. You girls make every day special. I love being your mother! Erin: Thank you for your suggestions and critiques. You are an excellent writer. Cam: Thank you for the "Keep Out While Mommy's Writing" sign on my office door. I know it was hard, but thanks for being patient with me throughout this process. I wrote this book for you girls so you'll always have an account of what our amazing God did for our entire family. Jesus rocks! I love you...more...just under Jesus.

To my mom and dad: I can't even imagine where I'd be without your unconditional love, patience, and hope. Thank you for never giving up on me—never. You've blessed me beyond measure, and I thank God for you. Dad, it's been hard, but I know God will bless you more than you can imagine someday. Mom, you are more like Jesus than anyone I know (except for HB, of course). For all the days you've taken care of me, I pray that I'll be blessed to do the same for you. You're an incredible woman. I love you both so much.

To my Hunterboy: Beyond words...immeasurably more than I could ever explain—I love you more than my heart can handle. See you soon, little buddy!

To Jesus: Nothing compares to You. You're it. You're everything. It's all for You, because my life and all that I am and have—it's all Yours. You're my heart's desire now and forever.

Appendix A

Hunter's Hope Foundation

Hunter's Hope Foundation was created to confront the critical need for information, awareness, and research in response to the threat of Krabbe disease and related Leukodystrophies. In addition, we strive to undergird and inspire Krabbe families as they adjust to the extreme demands of living with a terminal illness.

Our Mission

1. To broaden public awareness of Krabbe disease and other Leukodystrophies, thus increasing the odds of early detection and treatment.
2. To mount an aggressive public relations campaign throughout political, corporate, and private sectors in hopes of alerting key community leaders to the potential of newborn screening as a weapon in the fight against Krabbe disease.
3. To fund research efforts that will identify and develop new treatments, therapies, and ultimately a cure for Krabbe disease and related Leukodystrophies.

4. To establish an alliance of hope that will reach out to those directly and indirectly affected by Leukodystrophies, while addressing their urgent need for medical, financial, informational, and emotional support.

Among the primary goals of founders Jim and Jill Kelly is a hands-on appreciation for all children, along with a thankful heart toward God for these precious gifts of life. These bedrock ideals are vigilantly expressed throughout all the foundation's programs and activities.

Core Values

To remain true to and passionate about our bedrock principles.

To be sure our family-oriented, wholesome public image is simply a clear reflection of who we are privately.

To always value individual contributions and never take another's sacrifice for granted, no matter how large or small.

To pursue personal and professional integrity in all matters.

To hold the right of privacy of all individuals in the highest regard.

Krabbe Disease

Krabbe (crab ā) disease, known among the medical community as Globoid Cell Leukodystrophy, is an inherited neurodegenerative lysosomal enzyme disorder affecting the central and peripheral nervous systems. Children who inherit the illness lack an important enzyme (known as GALC) that is needed for the production of normal myelin (white matter) in the central and peripheral nervous systems. Myelin is critical because it acts as the protective covering of the nerve cells, much like the insulation that surrounds an electric wire. When the enzyme GALC is deficient, toxic substances are produced in the brain, causing myelin loss, change to brain cells, and neurological damage.

There are four types of Krabbe disease: early infantile, later onset infantile, adolescent, and adult. Progression of the disorder is rapid, causing death to occur in early childhood in the infantile Krabbe. It is found in all ethnic groups, and one in one hundred thousand live births in the United States are afflicted with Krabbe disease. Approximately 2 million people (or 1 out of 125) in the United States are carriers of the genetic deficiency that causes the disease. It is easy to diagnose, yet, as widespread as it is, awareness about this illness is very limited.

Until recently the only treatment options were limited to symptom management and palliative care. Now, a revolutionary treatment called a *cord blood transplant* is saving the lives of many young children and babies. This new method of treatment is bringing fresh hope to those afflicted with a variety of diseases including Krabbe, other Leukodystrophies, and Lysosomal Storage Disorders.

––––––––

Hunter's Hope Foundation is fully committed to providing encouragement, education, and support to our families. Our hope and prayer is that you will feel connected to our family and join us in this fight against these devastating diseases. In striving to achieve our mission, our Family Programs encompass key areas designed to meet the needs of our families.

Hunter's Homes

Since 2005, Hunter's Hope has been providing support to families when their child needs to be hospitalized at Duke Hospital in

Durham, North Carolina. A critical need for families when traveling to Durham from another city is being able to afford lodging accommodations for an undetermined length of time.

To lighten the financial burden, Hunter's Hope offers three completely furnished apartments called "Hunter's Homes," located in Durham approximately 4.7 miles from Duke Hospital. Our Hunter's Homes are accessible to any of our Leukodystrophy families (when available) while their child receives treatment (bone marrow or cord blood transplant, or pre- or post-transplant check-ups) at the hospital. Since we acquired the apartments, each unit has been occupied on a continual basis, with families staying from two weeks to one year. There is no charge for a family to stay. Donations are accepted if the family is able and desires to do so. It is our goal to provide families with a "home away from home" atmosphere during a very difficult time.

Family Care

Hunter's Hope is committed to encourage, support, and assist families throughout their journey. Having a support network is one of the most important resources a family needs during this trying time. When families are ready to connect with other families, Hunter's Hope can help bridge that support with other registered Krabbe and Leukodystrophy families. Our registry is used as a vehicle to introduce families to those living in closest proximity to their homes. It is a relief as well as an encouragement to speak with others who can relate to what your family is experiencing. In return, families may find themselves in a position someday where they can offer support to a family in need.

Families are also faced with questions regarding medical care. Hunter's Hope offers assistance by helping families connect with some of the most knowledgeable and world-renowned doctors. These doctors may offer assistance in treating a child or guide parents as to what is best for their child at that time. In addition, Family Care offers support in other areas through our Family Programs.

Equipment Exchange

Hunter's Hope equipment exchange is designed to help our Krabbe and Leukodystrophy children who have adaptive equipment needs. Once your child's equipment is no longer of service to him or her, please contact our *Director of Family Programs* to notify us of the available equipment. When another child needs the equipment, Hunter's Hope will pay the shipping fee to send this equipment to the new recipient family.

Hunter's Wish Gift

Definition of *wish*: *to have a desire or hope for something unattainable.*

A very special part of the Family Programs is our Hunter's Wish Gift. This gift is granted to a family with an apparent need. Recently, Hunter's Hope helped a family acquire an appropriate vehicle for their wonderful young son, Dalton, who requires transportation on a daily basis. With the foundation's assistance, Dalton's family purchased a handicapped-accessible conversion van. Through the continuous giving of our supporters, Hunter's Hope is honored to have helped Dalton's family with a gift that appeared "unattainable." We are trusting that we can help more families in the future.

What Is Universal Newborn Screening?

Universal Newborn Screening is a state-based public health system that is essential for preventing the devastating consequences of a number of medical conditions not clinically recognizable at birth. All babies born in the U.S. receive newborn screening, yet not all babies are screened for the same diseases. Because the newborn screening requirements differ from state to state and are not universal, children are not being checked for many rare diseases.

Thousands and thousands of babies are born every day in the United States. Most babies appear healthy at birth, full of life and possibility. Yet they could be hiding a rare or potentially devastating disease. By screening every baby at birth, we can prevent serious mental or physical disabilities, even death. Also, by making the requirement universal in every state, we can ensure that no child will have to suffer unnecessarily.

To learn more about Hunter's Hope, Krabbe disease, or Universal Newborn Screening, visit our website, www.huntershope.org.

Appendix B

The Hunter's Hope Kids

After news of Hunter's disease hit local and national media circuits, we were inundated with fan mail from all over the country. The outcry of support, get-well wishes, and prayers was astounding and encouraging. Through the thousands of letters, it soon became very apparent that we were not alone in our plight to help Hunter and kids like him. We had to do something.

We were also overwhelmed with media requests for television, print, and radio interviews. Everyone wanted to know what was wrong with Jim Kelly's son. Oprah wanted to know. *People* magazine wanted to know. ESPN wanted to know. We were determined to put a face on this horrible disease most people had never heard of. The world needed to know about Krabbe Leukodystrophy and other inherited neurodegenerative disorders. So in September 1997, when Hunter was eight months old, the Hunter's Hope Foundation was established.

I could share the unprecedented journey that our family has been on since the inception of Hunter's Hope, but I'm not going to do that. (However, if you're interested in learning more about the foundation and all that God is doing through Hunter's Hope, please visit our website at www.huntershope.org.) Instead, I'm going to introduce you to some special children I know and love dearly. I can't wait to tell you about these kids; they're amazing. I've had the incredible privilege of meeting many precious children over the past twelve years, and I love every one of them. I would love to share all their stories too, but that would fill at least a few more books.

We've been on an emotional roller-coaster ride over the years, and at times we've wanted to give up and walk away from it all. But we didn't and we won't. Determination and dedication continue to prevail even though discouragement and doubt always lurk nearby. When our weaknesses and inadequacies tempt us to throw in the towel, another beautiful child gets diagnosed with Krabbe disease and we press on. And Hunter's legacy lives on, beyond our hopes and dreams and by the grace of God, far beyond our vapor of life here on earth.

I continue to be in awe of how God has used our beloved son to spread hope, life, and love to countless people all over the country and the world. Yet just as inspiring are the children for whom we do what we do at Hunter's Hope. They take our breath away, and their very lives encourage each of us to be a better human being...a patient and gentle spouse...a more gracious and loving parent...a sincere friend...a good listener...and a person who loves deeper and forgives every time. Though most of these kids will slip in and out of our lives without ever speaking a single word, their lives are filled with a contagious love that speaks clearer and penetrates the soul deeper than words ever could. They're unforgettable, and I'd like you to meet some of them.

———

Mikey is from New Jersey. I was shocked when I saw him at the Hunter's Hope Family and Medical Symposium this year, because he had grown so much since the last time I laid eyes on him. He's a stocky young fellow now with leg muscles made for kicking soccer balls. His blond hair and blue eyes were as bright as ever, and Camryn was thrilled when she found out that he was coming, because it meant her best friend, Amanda (Mikey's older sister), was coming, too. When Cam and Amanda get together, you never see them. They're usually off somewhere having so much fun that we have to pry them away from each other at the end of the day. They have a lot in common, and walking through the Krabbe battle with a beloved sibling is at the top of that list.

Mikey usually hangs out with Chance and John. John didn't wear his vest this year, and everyone who knows him noticed. I heard a number of people ask him, "John, where's your cool vest? I was hoping to see a few new buttons this year." John's vest reminds me of a Boy Scout. It's covered in all sorts of pins and medals, honors only a cool boy like John and those who know and love him can fully appreciate.

When the boys get together, they usually hang out with their wheelchairs all lined up in a row next to each other near their moms and dads. They're affectionately known as "The Boys Club."

This year, little Miss Madison was the only girl with the courage to hang out with The Boys Club, and what a sight to see! We caught John trying to hold Madison's hand a few times even though he knows he's way too old for her. They all have Krabbe disease. And they all radiate a hope and joy uncommon in our world today.

Every year I get to hold and snuggle a few of the kids, and this year it was Elias, Chance, and Madison. Elias reminds me so much of Hunter when he was little, so holding him was a special treat that brought back many very personal memories. Once he was out of his wheelchair and into my arms, I didn't want our time together to end. I wanted him to fall asleep close to my heart like Hunter used to. Elias has long eyelashes and gentle brown eyes that penetrate your soul. He fit perfectly in my lap with his head tucked into the bend of my left arm. As I held him for as long as his mom and dad would let me, I ran my fingers through his soft brown hair and gently traced his eyebrows and little nose with my forefinger.

He reminds me so much of Hunter, and his birthday is in February, too. It's hard, but the joy of being a part of his life, even if only for a brief time, is worth it. Elias isn't quite old enough to be in The Boys Club yet, but he managed to get some quality time in with his buddies during his five-day stay at the symposium. Elias's mom and dad are crazy about him, and their fear of losing him is evident. He wasn't diagnosed with Krabbe disease early enough, so a cord blood transplant wasn't an option for him. I hope and pray he'll be back next year.

Chance is my buddy. I have watched him grow into a strong, handsome young man over the past four years. I was surprised at how mature and grown up he looked this year. Chance's birthday is the same day as my wedding anniversary, and he also reminds me of Hunter—when he was older. As I write this, "Chancey Pants" (his mom calls him that) is eight years old and thriving despite the countless hurdles Krabbe disease throws at him daily. He's a tough kid and, like most of the young fellas in The Boys Club, Chance was diagnosed with Krabbe at fourteen months— too late to get a transplant. But he's brave, and also like his pals, he continues to persevere in the battle for his life.

I could feel how much Chance grew over the last year when I held him in my lap. "Chance, you are getting so big," I told him. "What's your mommy feeding you anyway?"

Like Hunter, Chance learned how to communicate by blinking once for yes, and while he relaxed in my embrace we had a wonderful conversation. My fingers were drawn to his thick, brown, wavy hair, and my heart was his for a time. "Chance, your big-boy teeth remind me of Hunter. And I can tell you take such good care of them, right, Mommy?" He blinked, and I glanced over at his mother, Anne, and she smiled. Anne is tough and hopeful. She has no illusions about her son's prognosis, but Chance is so full of life and joy. So they courageously persevere...together. Hopefully he'll be back next year, too.

Hopefully they'll all be back.

Madison is from Rochester, New York. She's beautiful. Madison's mom always makes sure Madison is dressed in adorable girlie outfits, usually every shade of pink, yellow, and purple. And her shimmering blonde hair is often decorated with fancy barrettes, pigtails, or braids. Madison was born six months before New York State started testing newborns for Krabbe disease. Had she been tested at birth, she would've been eligible for a cord blood transplant, which would have made all the difference in the world. But she missed the test. And every single minute of every day she lives, it's a battle. And yet there's a radiance about her that is unmistakable.

In the midst of all the suffering these children endure, there is hope and peace. And the love that pours out of their parents is so abundant and unconditional. These are the kind of people you want to spend your time with, pour out your life for—you want to be like them because you know they're real and authentic. I'm so thankful God brought us together for such a time as this—to love, pray, laugh, and cry together, and to carry one another's burdens and extend a comfort only we can to each other because we've been there; we get it. It's extraordinary.

Gina, now she's a fireball. She's one of the funniest, spunkiest kids I know. Gina had a cord blood transplant when she was just three weeks old and she'll turn double digits, ten years old, a few days before Christmas this year. Her older brother Nick was also born with Krabbe disease, but there was no treatment or newborn screening available for him in 1986, so he died at twelve months. She never got to meet her brother, but she will someday.

Even though Gina can't do everything kids her age can, she's a typical kid who just happens to need a little extra help to function on a daily basis.

I watched her dance around and around in her bright pink power wheelchair in front of the family audience for the Symposium Family Talent Show. Her song of choice was "Camp Rock" from the popular Disney movie. Her nails were painted bright pink to complement her sparkly bracelets and glittery Camp Rock t-shirt. Gina loves to dance, even if only in her wheelchair. Hope radiates from her contagious smile, and you can't help but rejoice whenever you're around her.

I e-mailed Gina's mom, Anne, today to let her know that I was writing about her daughter, and after reading her response, my heart was so full that I just had to share what she said:

I prayed for you before I ever knew you, Jim, Hunter, and your family . . . after Nick was diagnosed on December 23, 1986. (Gina was born December 23, 1999, thirteen years later.) I was told that I would never meet another family with Krabbe, nor would there ever be any medical treatments for children born with Krabbe. I knew at that moment that it would take a family with great love and a much higher profile to be affected by this dreadful disease to prove those doctors wrong. I know that you and Jim were chosen for this endeavor to enlighten the world about Krabbe, and to also bring hope through Jim's successes—and your inspiration and love—to save all of the children born with Krabbe and other rare genetic diseases. I knew that God would send someone to help our

*children—another child to bring some hope to other families
and other children. I thank God for Hunter and your family.*

*That's what Hunter's Hope is all about. The children and their
families, the heartbreak and the hope.*

Gina and her girlfriend Laura are like sisters whenever they
get together at the symposium. Laura is adorable and super-sweet.
Although she and Gina have different personalities and unique
interests, they have some very important things in common.
Like Gina, Laura had a cord blood transplant, and she, too, has
a brother in heaven. His name is Joshua and, like Gina, Laura
never met her big brother either. But someday she will. If her
brother were alive today, he would be seventeen years old.

Laura participated in the talent show this year as well. After her
daddy helped her prepare on stage, Laura played a song on her lap
harp: "The Ants Go Marching." But she changed the title to "The
Cats Go Marching." A look of pride blushed over Laura's face when
she finished her song and we all erupted with applause and praise.

These kids are amazing. None of them should be here right
now. They have Krabbe disease. Kids who suffer from Krabbe
don't participate in talent shows; they can't dance and sing and
play. And yet they can and do. Because by God's grace there's a
cord blood transplant now; there's a treatment for this horrify-
ing, life-stealing disease. There's hope! And that's why there's
Hunter's Hope.

You can't be around the Hunter's Hope kids and not catch a
wave of their determination, joy, and courageous spirit. And to
think that tragedy and suffering brought us together to form an
unlikely bond that will endure beyond our lifetimes...it's irra-
tional and immeasurably more than all we would've imagined or
hoped for. It's an unspoken love without boundaries that mends
brokenness and severs barriers. Extraordinary!

Hunter needed a miracle. Or maybe he was the miracle. Because from his life was borne a greater life that reaches out and rescues hopeless families and countless children we'll never know.

That's our hope and our future. And maybe that's what God meant (as it pertains to Hunter, our family, and all who are touched through Hunter's Hope) when in the Old Testament book of Jeremiah He proclaimed, "'For I know the plans I have for you' declares the LORD, 'plans to prosper you and not to harm you, plans to give you hope and a future'" (Jer. 29:11).

We're hopeful…very hopeful…that our future is secure and safe in the hands of a mysterious God whose love is constant even when we don't always understand His ways. That's our hope and future. How else can you explain the incredible hope that blossomed from a child's suffering?

It's indescribable. And I suppose it should be, since the little boy behind it all never spoke a word. Yet his unspoken love… changed everything.

Appendix C

"Team Hunter" Memories

Dear Hunter,

I praise God for each and every moment I was blessed to be in your presence. Each memory that I have with you is so special to me.

One day that I will never forget is August 3, 2005. I had been praying to spend more time with you, and God answered this prayer in the most amazing way, as only He can. Instead of doing Kingdom Bound during the day, Mommy asked me to spend Monday and Wednesday with my little buddy. I have to tell you that there is no other place I would have rather been than with you.

I loved listening to Mommy and Daddy on FLN with you and Ellen. I know you enjoyed listening to them in Noah's ark and hearing Mommy's adventure with her water bottle.

I'll never forget you, Ellen, and I going out onto the deck, waiting for Grammie to come home. Ellen and I hid behind the grill so that Grammie only saw you as she walked up to the door. How surprised she was to see you outside by yourself! (Of course, Ellen and I popped out of our hiding spot shortly after she saw you.)

I love how you moved your feet for us, Hunter. We told you which one to move, and you wiggled it. Thank you so much for showing us all the wonderful things God helped you do!

Hunter, I also want to thank God for His mercies that are new every day. He is so amazing! Before I left that day, I waited to ask Grammie a question and I walked over to you three times to give you a kiss and run my hands through your hair. I just love how God cares so much to arrange such a special moment for me.

Even though that was the last moment I spent with you here on earth, I know I will see you again in heaven. Thank you for all the laughter and smiles you brought to everyone!

I love you, Hunter. See you soon!

Love, "Jennyfer"
(A dear friend and nanny)

Dear Hunter,

Looking back, I have so many "favorite" memories of you. I remember many times that I sat with you while you were taking your bath and I got to watch you show off by moving your head. I remember watching your eyes light up when Mommy walked into the room or you heard her voice. Prayer parties with you were some of my favorite times! I loved worshiping Jesus with you.

I will never forget the time that we let you taste a candy cane and you bit it off! We didn't know what to do, and we had to figure out a way to get it out of your mouth, silly boy. I loved playing with your soft, curly hair or lying down next to you on the bed while you were watching Rescue Heroes, and I loved building the ceramic volcano with you. But the memory that sticks out most to me was that day in Ellicottville in July 2005. Your whole family was at the symposium and it was just you, me, and Ellen at the lodge.

Ellen asked me to watch you while she took care of something, so I was able to just hang out with you for a little bit. I remember talking, laughing, playing a game and singing Bible songs. You probably thought I was crazy, but I remember the happiness in your eyes because it equaled the joy in my heart. I am so thankful that God gave us that time together.

Hunter, without you in my life, I would not be the same person that I am today and I praise God for your influence. Thank you for teaching me what it means to live. Living does not always mean accomplishing everything on your to-do list, but it is learning to love. Thank you for causing me to slow down and enjoy the moment. Thank you for stretching me beyond my comfort zone and teaching me what selflessness really means. Thank you for teaching me what it means to serve like Jesus calls us to serve—in humility. You helped me to discover how to be more like Him every day.

I still have so much to learn, but your life caused me to evaluate mine and to decide how I want to live it. You encouraged me to claim my faith as my own and to wholly and completely surrender my life to Jesus Christ. Losing you broke my heart, but I have watched God mend it and bring healing to my life. Thank you for loving me enough to challenge me to be more like Jesus. Hunter, thank you for teaching me how to live. I'll see you soon, bud. Soon and very soon.

Cassie
(A dear friend and nanny)

A memory is a picture in your mind. I have a beautiful memory of some very quiet moments with Hunter. These moments were on Good Friday two years ago (2003). It was between 12:00 and 3:00 p.m., the hours Jesus was on the cross. I had the privilege of being able to read to Hunter about the Easter story. He was on his mat in the living room, and I sat down right next to him. As I read to him and held his hand, I felt a sense of peace like I had never felt before. It was very, very quiet. Only Hunter and I were home at the time.

I remember telling him about how, when I was a child, we read the Easter story on Good Friday between 12:00 and 3:00 p.m. and then went to church to ring the bell thirty-three times. This was at 3:00 p.m. when Jesus said, "It is finished," and died. The thirty-three times symbolized how long He lived here on earth.

I remember telling Hunter how much Jesus loves him and how much He loves each and every one of us, and how this "darkest day in all the world" was only temporary. As we talked, he listened. Hunter's gentle spirit filled the room and filled my heart. His precious, precious breathing filled my ears like the most beautiful music I had ever heard. It was as though Hunter wanted to tell me, "Oh, Ellen—I know that darkest day was only temporary. The miracle of Jesus rising from the dead on Easter was just one of the many continuous miracles of life. He gave His all for us and still does this today." And Hunter told me with his sweet eyes that it's always going to be okay.

I'm so thankful that I have these Good Friday moments to treasure forever. God gave me the beautiful privilege of sharing so many moments with you, Hunter.

Love,
Ellen
(Hunter's RN)

I have so many wonderful memories of Hunter. It was very difficult to pick just one to share. I finally decided to recall the first lesson I taught him. Although it wasn't the first time we had met, it was our first official day as student/teacher. I can remember him sitting so proudly in his chair, wrapped in his Scooby Doo blanket and wearing his Buffalo Bills hat. He welcomed me with a look I shall never forget. It was a look of a child who had a desire to learn.

We worked outside on the deck and I taught him about apples. We read a book about Johnny Appleseed, cut an apple in half to make star prints with paint, and made a mobile of an apple as it was being eaten out of foam. At the end of the lesson Hunter used a highlighter to trace his name with assistance, and then on his own he drew a picture. During the entire lesson, he was so interested in hearing everything I had to say. I could tell with each sentence that he was eager to hear more. Hunter was so cooperative and so willing to allow hand-over-hand assistance. He was so determined to complete each task I gave him.

Hunter really seemed to enjoy our time together that day, as did I. I knew it was a match made in heaven. I thank God so often for the honor of being handpicked by Him to be Hunter's second-grade teacher. I shall always and forever treasure my time with him. Although Hunter was the "student" and I was the "teacher," many times I left your home feeling like I was the student. Your son taught me so much about life, about God, and about himself. Jill, thank you for allowing me to teach Hunter and for sharing him with me.

Love,
Bonnie
(Hunter's favorite teacher)

Wisdom is so misunderstood in our world today. Hunter was a child who was never confused about what it means to be truly wise. He knew what God's plan was for his life, and he did God's will here on earth with humility and great understanding. How blessed I have been to be able to witness such wisdom in such a young child.

I am thankful for the experience of being able to touch, hold, and learn from a child whose body was so wise. To be trusted and guided by his little body when he was just a few months old was profound. With awe and amazement I continued to observe his body grow in wisdom and understanding of what he needed to do on this earth until he was called home to heaven. What a lesson Hunter and his family taught me about using every gift you have been given, every day, to its fullest, to do our Lord's will. I have learned that this is what it means to be truly wise.

My mind and heart are filled with memories of my buddy Hunter, watching him grow from an infant into a beautiful child, watching his family (who were chosen specifically for him) train up their child in the way he should go, and experiencing life with a team and family who have changed me as a therapist, wife, mother, and daughter of God. It takes someone full of wisdom to change lives. God in His wisdom chose a child. He chose Hunter James Kelly. God is good.

"Who is wise and understanding among you? Let him show it by his good life, by deeds done in the humility that comes from wisdom" (James 3:13).

"The fear of the LORD is the beginning of wisdom; all who follow his precepts have good understanding. To him belongs eternal praise" (Psalm 111:10).

Memories:

Hunter sleeping in his crib.

*Quiet time together on Saturday mornings in Hunter's
bedroom upstairs.*
Massaging Hunter's legs and feet.
Hunter moving his arms up and down over and over again.
Hunter's patience when adjusting his Kid Kart.
Hunter's first time in his stander.
*Hunter's faith when he was "jumpy" and I was at a loss
about what to do to help him.*
Hunter's enjoyment when watching squirrels.
Butterscotch (when she was a puppy) lying next to Hunter.
Hunter's music.
Hunter's sense of humor.

> All my love,
> Kathy
> (Hunter's occupational therapist)

The best memory of Hunter that I can share is the last
night I spent with him. Here are my thoughts. . . .

I didn't know why at the time, but God placed it on my
heart to work the overnight shift on Wednesday, August 3,
from 10:00 p.m. to 10:00 a.m. Looking back, it was a blessing and God's hand was upon us that night.

Hunter had mucus plugs that blocked his airways at midnight and 1:00 a.m. Grammie was there to help me, and he
started breathing again after suctioning, repositioning, and
increasing his oxygen (his oxygen saturation was in the 20s).

I constantly talked to Hunter for the next two hours,
softly reminding him to take "Reggie" breaths so I could give
her a good report when she asked me about him, and to reassure him that I was still there. During this time I quietly read
his prayer journal to him, not once but twice! I also put a

couple new entries into his journal, the last one being from
1 Peter 1:3–4 . . . a gift from God to Hunter and you and
me: "In his great mercy he has given us new birth into a living hope . . . from the dead, and into an inheritance that can
never perish, spoil or fade—kept in heaven for you."

We also prayed a lot that night. I put my hands on Hunter
and prayed each time before I repositioned him, asking God
to help the transition go well and to help Hunter continue
breathing. He answered my prayers and Hunter was able to
relax and fall asleep around 3:30 a.m.

I am also thankful that my husband got to meet Hunter
on Thursday morning. He rode to Grammie's house with
Ellen so he could drive me home from working the night shift.
He came into the house and said, "Hi, Hunter." I always
talked to Hunter about Mr. Warner and showed him pictures
of his marathon, and now he got to meet him face-to-face.
What a blessing that was for John and me!

I am so thankful to God for allowing me that special
night, one-on-one with Hunter. He knew that would be my
last time with him, and He made it so special!

> Love and Blessings,
> Barb
> (Hunter's RN)

Today has been filled with thoughts of you and your son, so
this present has been a joy to assemble. The picture of your son
was taken on another birthday—Hunter and Jim's—when that
little preschooler was determined to make a delicious cake for
his dad. As usual, Hunter was not thinking about himself, but
about how he could bring joy to someone else. Marion [Hunter's
teacher at the time] and I worked for about two hours to get

everything just right, and he totally loved digging right in with both hands. What a fabulous day that was, and what insight it provided into your son's personality. How many times I would witness that love and determination over the years, and how many times it would spark love and determination in others.

Hunter was with us throughout this special day today. This morning, the biggest dragonfly ever perched itself on our kitchen screen for several hours, allowing us to observe it from all angles and notice how amazingly complex and beautiful it is. Robert said that he thought Hunter would really like the dragonfly because he likes bugs so much.

I shared with Robert this morning the memory of Hunter baking. Robert and I then baked your cake, which is an exact replica of that birthday cake baked several years ago by Hunter himself, although it is quite a bit bigger. This has become Hunter's cake, and I'm enclosing the recipe for your enjoyment. Robert mixed the cake with the big mixer and not his hands because that would be the way that Hunter would do it now that he is eight. We sang Hunter's favorite songs and wanted to make the cake as beautiful and delicious as we could to honor his memory.

Robert decided on the cake's decoration himself, again thinking about what Hunter would want to do for his mom on her special day. He wanted the Hunter's Hope insignia and also to put "Trust in God" on the cake. The Hunter's Hope insignia is, of course, green because of "hunter green," and the writing is in red to represent Hunter's sometimes-favorite color and the blood of Christ. The gold sprinkles represent the riches Hunter has received in heaven—riches that await us all if we only trust in Him.

Most of all, Jill, I want you to know that we are continuing to build memories of Hunter. We felt his love and presence here today, as I know you do every minute of every day.

*We thank you for sharing the gift of Hunter with us and hope
our memory fills your heart with the love we feel for your son.*

> *With Hope,*
> *Elizabeth* (Hunter's physical therapist)
> *and Robert* (Hunter's best friend)
> *September 9, 2005*

My Memories of Hunter

*There are so many . . . where do I start? It is hard to
find the right words for what my special, quality time with
Hunter was all about. I can start by saying that Hunter was
a teacher and a student, thoughtful and patient, courageous
and joyful. Six years is a long time to spend with such a special person, yet the years went so fast. Because Hunter loved
to learn, my list of memories is practically endless. I wanted
to write down a few of our special moments.*

*When I arrived at Hunter's house, I was pretty nervous
and I kept thinking to myself: I hope I say the right things to
him and I hope he can trust me. It didn't take long to realize that Hunter was a three-year-old little boy who wanted
to explore and learn. During our first year together, we tried
every switch toy we could get our hands on and picked out
his favorite computer games. He loved toys that made noise
(not too loud, though—he told me that right away), and he
loved the good old-fashioned learning toys. One of Hunter's
favorite games was when I set a race-car track on his shoulder and together we would make the car go downhill. It
didn't take long to realize that Hunter loved to learn about
opposites (up and down; stop and go).*

*Once Hunter told me with his eyes that he was comfortable
with any challenging activity, we moved on to shaving cream*

games, pudding games, cotton balls, and feathers. The feathers: that was Hunter's chance to show everyone how much air he could get into his lungs! We would take turns blowing, and he would always blink for enjoyment with that game.

Special moments between Hunter and I always surfaced when something I brought was a little more challenging. When he was four years old, we moved into many crafts. Boy, was Hunter an artist. Whenever someone would take a peek at our activity for the day, whether it was painting, coloring, or gluing, a look would come across their face as if to say, "Can Hunter really do this?" He always surprised everyone with his creative use of his hands, arms, shoulders, and even elbows.

Hunter even wrote many book reports, as he was ready to enter his school years. He loved making a picture to illustrate the story he had just read.

Hunter loved making gifts for Mommy and cards for everyone. His gifts always came from the heart, even if he needed a little help with the materials. He enjoyed making sunflowers for Mommy and special poems for Daddy. He always made time to make cards for his sisters too.

As Hunter's school years began, he proved to everyone that he could learn school-age material, just in a different way. The way he answered questions so consistently and effortlessly is a very special memory I keep in my mind. Hunter would always be calm and at ease when it was time to learn, even if he was having a difficult day with his breathing.

I feel like Hunter and I shared so much. But the most important memory that I will keep in my heart is that Hunter was a teacher. When I walked into Hunter's house for the first time, I was thinking, I am his teacher and I will teach him so much. But what I didn't realize is that Hunter was my teacher too. He taught me how to be brave in difficult times;

*how to encourage others to keep learning, and you can always
learn more; how to love people closest to you because no
one knows you better than they do; never take your days for
granted—there is always a challenge lying ahead; your children come first when you get home, and don't lose precious
time; and to always have hope for the days that lie ahead.*

*I miss Hunter deeply, and it is very difficult to change
a routine that I had with one of my closest friends after six
years. But I do know that it was a great privilege and honor
to get to know Hunter in such a special way.*

I will never forget you, Hunter.

Love,
Kristin
(Hunter's speech therapist)

*Wow! There are so many memories of Hunter that I cherish!
Some are when Hunter received the coveted Boy Scout Award;
just hanging out, praying, or reading to him at home; watching
him with you, Jill, on his first horse ride; and of course, getting
to hold him in the swimming pool at Grammie's. Although all of
these and tons more are precious, one that stands out the most
for me at this time is the "late night with Hunterboy" memory.*

*Everyone was settled down for the night. We all said
Scriptures together and prayed. What amazing times! Hunter
had his therapy and had finished watching a video . . . probably Young Black Stallion or Joseph. While you were getting ready for bed, Hunter and I talked about our day. He
had the usual busy day with therapy, school, playtime, and
Jacuzzi. Hunter should have been tuckered out big-time. I
was asking him so many questions and he was so talkative, it
just cracked me up! We laughed together as we talked about*

the Night Creatures story we'd read earlier in the playroom. We laughed a lot because Kimmy tried to draw some of those creatures after we read about them. Hunter was telling me what else I should draw or how I could make it look even better. He was so patient with me.

As we were discussing more of our day, you came into the room and told Hunter, "It's time to go to sleep, young man. It's almost one in the morning." You asked Hunter if he was ready for his eye band, and he said he wasn't. Then he told you that he did not want to go to sleep, but he wanted to stay up with us and talk. So talk we did. I said that I knew I was a night owl, but didn't know that he was. By his blinking, he told me he was a night bat because that was more boyish. (We'd read about owls and bats earlier that day.)

We asked if he wanted to stay up so he wouldn't miss anything that was happening, and he said yes! This may have been the same night of the counting and toe/foot moving game too. He wanted to stay awake to entertain us and hear our laughter. I think he was laughing pretty hard inside too.

Hunter was so funny and brought joy to my life. I remember all the serious, intense times of prayer and encouragement, but I love to recall all the times he made me laugh. This account is just one of so many. Life is not the same without my little buddy, but he lives on in my heart forever.

Love Always,
Kimmy
(A dear friend and nanny)

My favorite memories of Hunter are times when I got to watch Hunter when the nurses needed a break. I loved to talk to him and sing to him. I loved to look in his beautiful eyes and *tell him how special he was and still is. I also have wonderful memories of doing kids' church, arts and crafts, baking, and going for walks with Hunter. I could go on and on. He is a little warrior for God. I will always love him. Psalm 116:15— "Precious in the sight of the LORD is the death of his saints."*

Love, Jessica
(My cousin and dear friend)

My most vivid memories of Hunter involve his acceptance and unconditional love of all those around him. He appreciated everything anyone did for him. This even included my singing worship songs, which he always so graciously endured whenever I was able to sit with him. I also enjoyed those special times when I read him Bible stories, and I was always happy to help him and Aunt Dodie select his outfit for the day.

But perhaps one of my favorite remembrances of Hunter involves his sense of humor. This wonderful gift from God enabled Hunter and all of us to get through some of those tough days.

Hunter was and is a special child of God. In his own quiet way, he communicated mightily. He had a way of pointing me to Jesus without saying anything. It was actually through this "silence" that he spoke volumes, as God's still small voice was able to transcend Hunter's earthly limitations. I do believe the Holy Spirit moved through him, touching me and all with whom he came in contact. What a vehicle for God's love Hunter became!

Love, Karen
(Housecleaner, friend, and
whatever else we needed)

Appendix D

Hot Chocolate with God

Camryn was six years old when her older brother, Hunter, went to heaven. As a result of this loss, Camryn began at an early age to express her heart and grief through writing and continues to do so now. Camryn's original journal entries are a testimony to the faithfulness and gracious heart of a good and loving God.

We have compiled Camryn's journal entries into a book-like format and have titled her work *Hot Chocolate with God*. Camryn began writing *Hot Chocolate with God* in her Hello Kitty notebooks and sparkly journals during her journey of grief.

While she eloquently and freely exposes her struggles and fears, Camryn also shares her joy and hope. Her writing is filled with childlike faith and silly girl talk, and yet the profound truths woven throughout are clearly from the throne of grace.

While she is uninhibited in her approach and very elementary in style, her writing reaches into places most people run from. And though she is young, it's obvious that God has given Camryn a message to share with children her age...and grown-ups who are smart enough to understand. (To read more from *Hot Chocolate with God*, you can visit www.hotchocolatewithgod.com.)

I Am Free to Run!

We are free to run.
We are free to run with God today.
When we get to heaven we will run free.
And horses run free forever in heaven.
I am free to run, God.
I am free!
We are free in You, Lord.
God will let us go free.
We will take off the chains of hell and run free.
When we ask God into our heart we are free.
We are free to run in heaven.
God, we are free today.
We should say all the time, we are free.
Don't let sin get you, just say, I'm free to run!
I love You, God, so much.
Free, free, free.
We will open the gates and run free!
We are saved in God and free.

Day by Day

Day by day we pray with God and talk to Him.
Day by day we say thank You, God, for the things we have.
Day by day I worship You and my family does too.
Day by day we think of my brother Hunter and pray.
Day by day we read the Bible.
Day by day we pray for people.
Day by day we have faith.

Heart

Our heart is full of things.
Our heart is full of God.
Our heart is beating so fast.
Our heart is important to God.
Our heart has God in it and everything that we love.
My family is in my heart forever but most of all God
is in my heart.
Our heart is as red as Jesus' blood.
Our heart is full of love.
Our heart has sin in it.
But God changes our heart.
He makes our heart pure white.

God

God will save us from all fear.
God will help me.
God will save me.
God will teach me to read more of His Word in the Bible.
I will believe in God.
I love God.
I love God so much because He died for us and for
our sins on the cross.
He loves us.
God knows every thought in our head.
He teaches us to pray for people.
He loves us.
God, will You help me to know You more each and every day?
God will help me to grow.
God is amazing.

Tears

When we cry, we are sad.
We have tears of joy too.
Did you know that it's okay to cry?
It's okay to cry.
When I am sad, I cry.
But God knows that our tears can be happy tears too.
God has a bottle and He catches our tears in His bottle.
Tears are joyful and happy.
Tears, tears, tears are good.
I love tears.
It's okay to cry every day if you have to.

Thoughts

My thoughts these days are just not godly.
But, I know that God will change my heart and that He is
preparing a place for me in heaven.
I know that full well.

God Speaks to You

God speaks to you and says—you are Mine; no one can
snatch you away from Me.
God can speak to you through His Word.
We speak to Him through prayer.
When you are afraid, just talk to God and He will help you.
You can trust God. He will help you get through tough times,
so you can be happy and have a joyful heart.
God will speak to you and say—child, don't be afraid.
You can say to God—help me get through tough times with
my friends because I love them too much.

And I love you even more, God, and I know You will work
it all out and help me get through hard times.
God will speak to you and say—don't be afraid, just trust in
Me and you will be fine. And you will have a great life on
earth and in heaven.

Dear God

I love You so much.
How do You make everything so beautiful?
It's amazing!
I love You, Lord, and I will praise You forever.
And when I am in trouble You will help me.
I need You, God, to help me get through life.
And I hope You will cherish me forever in Your heart.
You spoke to everyone and said—
You are mine forever and ever.
You will never leave me nor forsake me.
I love You too much to let go of You, Lord.
You are my best friend and will always be my One and
Only.
You made the stars and the sky.
And You made us so beautiful and handsome.

I Love You!

Lord, You made the heavens and the earth.
I love You more than anything!
Love, Camryn Kelly

Appendix E

Jim Kelly's Hall of Fame Induction Speech

It's only fitting that I would follow Marv Levy. For years people have always credited me with being the leader of the Bills, but I can honestly tell you, the real leader for our great teams is that man right there, Marv Levy.

Congratulations to my fellow inductees. It is truly a great honor to be here today. I have had the distinct pleasure of playing on some pretty good football teams. Today, I join the greatest team of them all—the Pro Football Hall of Fame.

My life has been a series of crossing patterns involving family and football. I can't remember a time when football hasn't been a part of my life. But I can tell you I never would have made it this far without the constant love, support, and dedication of my family, friends, and you—the Buffalo Bills fans...the greatest fans in the NFL.

The head coach is the leader of the team, and my dad has been the best head coach a family could ever have. This is a man who taught us that dedication carries its own reward. This was a tough lesson to learn, especially during those few times when I was hiding at the neighbors' to avoid one of his daily passing drills for me at lunch and after school.

It has been written throughout my career that toughness is my trademark. Growing up with five brothers, you learn at an early age that you need to be tough to survive. Not only on the field, but at the dinner table.

Of course, we might have thought we were tough, but the toughest Kelly of them all was my mother, Alice, or "St. Alice," as we always called her. She did everything from putting food on our personal training table to scrubbing all our uniforms, including those of many of our teammates. On more than one occasion she told people: "I wouldn't trade my boys for the world, but there were days where I would have gladly given them away." My mother had tremendous pride in all of her sons, and I know she is smiling down on all of us today.

My oldest brother, Pat, taught me about hard work and has always provided wisdom and advice. Pat has written me letters since my college days. They congratulated me in times of victory and inspired me in times of trouble. He has always been the real field general amongst the Kelly brothers.

My brother Ed was the original quarterback of the family. Quiet and smart... and something he's never known... he's a part of the reason I chose to be a quarterback.

I could always count on my brother Ray to be my honest critic. He always told it the way it was, never sugarcoating anything. Thanks, Ray. I appreciate your straightforward comments more than you'll ever know.

My twin brothers, Danny and Kevin, have physically been with me every step of the way. Danny has been my most trusted confidant. To this day, I trust no one like I trust Danny.

Kevin is without a doubt my biggest fan. After signing autographs for Kevin for years, I finally asked one day, "Who are these for, Kevin?" He smiled and said, "They're for me, bro."

I learned the importance of extended family as early as Midget football, where men like Art Delano, Gary Faust, Jim Martin, and Jimmy King were more than coaches. They gave me the guidance that went well beyond the football field. I will never forget Art Delano sitting with me in his personal sauna, his Volkswagen Beetle, with the windows rolled up on a hot summer day after we had just run alongside the railroad tracks and the Allegheny River in order for me to make playing weight. While my friends rode mini-bikes and went swimming, this is where I learned all about sacrifice.

When you grow up in the hotbed of high school football, you live the game as much as you play it. And believe me, the East Brady Bulldogs ate, slept, and drank football. Terry Henry, our coach, was a jack-of-all-trades. He was our trainer, equipment manager, teacher, counselor, and father all rolled into one for not only myself and my brothers, but teammates like Jimmy Hiles, Kevin Morrow, and Paul DeBacco. And, Terry, the fact that you remain close to our family to this day speaks volumes. You will always be a key ingredient to why I made it as far as I did.

Coach Howard Schnellenberger's arrival to the University of Miami was a godsend for me. He was a drill sergeant, a hard-nosed coach—something that every cocky high school athlete needed. Especially me. And with him came Earl Morrall, who taught me how to read defenses.

After injuring my shoulder in my senior year, I was told that I would never play again. But our trainer, Mike O'Shea, and my best friend and college roommate, Mark Rush, had different thoughts. They worked me through countless hours of rehab to get me healthy enough to fulfill my dream of playing professional football. Thanks, guys, especially you, Roomie. To Art Kehoe, Don Bailey, Tony Fitzpatrick, and so many others, thanks for being much more than just Hurricane teammates.

I entered the USFL's Houston Gamblers as a quarterback and left as a passer. Head Coach Jack Pardee gave us direction and

Mouse Davis taught me the art of the passing game. It may have lasted only a brief time, but the run-and-shoot was around long enough to make an impact in my professional career. Throwin' was never as much fun.

And then I made the greatest decision of my life—I became a Buffalo Bill.

I can't think of a better owner to play for than Ralph Wilson, and his place in this Hall is waiting. He guaranteed me that he would provide the weapons for the Bills to be a Super Bowl team, and boy, did he ever.

Future Hall of Famers Thurman Thomas, I don't know where I would have been without number 34...Bruce Smith, thank God Bruce was on my team...Andre Reed, 12+83=???...James Lofton, the best deep threat in the game...and the greatest special teams player ever, Steve Tasker...not to mention Darryl Talley...Jim Richter...Will Wolford...Pete Metzelaars...Don Beebe, another great deep threat...my personal coach in a jersey, Frank Reich... and the real reason the no-huddle offense thrived the way it did, MY center, MY friend, and a great leader, Kent Hull.

Man, talk about egos...We went through some growing pains early on, didn't we, Thurm? But we always knew that to succeed, we had to do it together. Four consecutive Super Bowls...I think we can safely say that we did it together.

As Chris Berman always tells us, "NO ONE...circles the wagons...like the Buffalo Bills." Our Bills family was as close as could be. Bill Polian put us together...John Butler kept us together...and Marv Levy saw to it that we played together. Marv, never have so many eloquent words been wasted on a bunch of guys who always chose SportsCenter over your History Channel. How about that, Marv? I used "eloquent" in a sentence! Bruce, did you get that?

The phrase "no-huddle" became a household name in Western New York but would never have been possible without offensive coordinator Ted Marchibroda, who trusted his quarterback to call all of his own plays. Thanks, Ted. In addition to Ted were Tom Bresnahan, Jim Shofner, the late, great Elijah Pitts, and many others. Job well done, men.

There are so many others in the Bills family that I represent today, but a special thanks to Scott Berchtold, Rusty Jones, Ed Abramoski, Bud Carpenter, Woody, and Hojo. I could write a complete speech on these six men. But they know where their place is in my heart.

I also want to take this opportunity to thank the Hall of Fame Selection Committee, especially Larry Felser and Vic Carucci. And there are others who have touched my life... like Tommy Good, my daughter's godfather and the seventh Kelly brother. The parties at my house after the game would not have been the same without you, buddy.

Finally, I want to thank my immediate family—my three amazing children, Erin, Hunter, and Camryn; and my wife, Jill. Jill is the backbone and spiritual rock of the Kelly household. Her faith and her unselfishness make her the kind of mother every father wants for their children. She is Mother of the Year every day of her life.

When I announced my retirement on January 31, 1997, we were already blessed with a beautiful daughter named Erin, the next Olympic swimmer. Two weeks later, on Valentine's Day, our son was born... on Daddy's birthday. I dreamt what every father dreams about... playing catch in the backyard, going fishing, camping, and all the great things that fathers and sons do. But within four months my son was diagnosed with a fatal disease—Krabbe Leukodystrophy. Now we're all fighting for his life.

It has been written throughout my career that toughness is my trademark. But the toughest person I've ever met is my hero, my soldier, my son, Hunter. I love you, buddy.

Thank you, Canton, and God bless you.

Notes

Chapter 11: Hunter at Seven

    1. *Webster's New World Dictionary,* 3rd College Ed. (New York: Simon & Schuster, Inc., 1991).

Chapter 15: Unexpected Grace

    1. Randy Alcorn, *Heaven* (Carol Stream, IL: Tyndale House, 2004), 55.

    2. Ibid., 70.

    3. Ibid., 73.

Chapter 17: Walking Through the Valley

    1. Verses have been personalized by the author.

Prayers of Hope for the Brokenhearted

Sometimes the deepest hurts are the most difficult to express. Times of grief and sorrow can also be times of great loneliness, when it seems we bear unbearable burdens by ourselves.

Jill Kelly's infant son, Hunter, was diagnosed with a terminal illness. During the difficult months that followed, Jill often wrote prayers in her journals. She poured out her anguish, pain, and questions to the One who could comfort, heal, and mend her broken heart. It was through the grace of a compassionate God that Jill found lasting hope and peace.

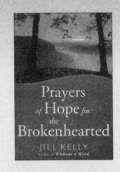

Prayers of Hope for the Brokenhearted is a collection of simple prayers that offer solace to anyone who experiences heartache and sorrow.

ISBN 978-0-7369-2933-2

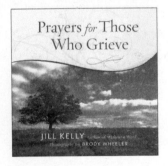

Prayers for Those Who Grieve

Jill Kelly knows the sorrow of loss. After burying her 8-year-old son, Hunter, she spent countless days and nights expressing her grief to God in her tear-stained journals and watching Him turn that grief into peace. In this gift book of comfort, Jill's prayers for those who journey through grief are accompanied by inspiring photographs of nature by award-winning professional photographer Brody Wheeler.

With a heart of compassion and deep empathy, Jill shares a message of hope for those who weep, those struggling to find words for their emotions, and for all who carry burdens they long to bring to God.

ISBN 978-0-7369-2934-9

HARVEST HOUSE PUBLISHERS

EUGENE, OREGON

www.harvesthousepublishers.com